# Who
# Am I
# This Time?

By the Same Author

*Winter Dreams: An American in Moscow*
*Always Merry and Bright: The Life of Henry Miller*
*Robert Lowell*
*Nathanael West: The Art of His Life*
*Harvests of Change: American Literature 1865–1914*
*Conrad Aiken: A Life of His Art*

# Who
# Am I
# This Time?

**W · W · NORTON & COMPANY**
*New York    London*

# Who
# Am I
# This Time?

*Uncovering
the Fictive Personality*

## JAY MARTIN

Some material in this book, published in somewhat different form, was awarded the Fritz Schmidl Memorial Prize, the Marie H. Briel Prize in Child Analysis, and the Franz Alexander Award. The author is grateful to the awarding committees for their encouragement.

The title of this book is derived from the short story "Who Am I This Time?" by Kurt Vonnegut, copyright Kurt Vonnegut, Jr., 1968. Permission for use has been granted by Donald C. Farber, Esq., of Tanner Gilbert Propp & Sterner, attorney for Mr. Vonnegut.

The poem "A Letter from Li Po" by Conrad Aiken is from *Collected Poems* by Conrad Aiken. Copyright (©) 1953, 1970 by Conrad Aiken; renewed 1981 by Mary Aiken. Reprinted by permission of Oxford University Press, Inc.

Published simultaneously in Canada by Penguin Books Canada Ltd., 2801 John Street, Markham, Ontario L3R 1B4.
Printed in the United States of America.

The text of this book is composed in Janson, with display type set in ITC Isbell Medium.
Composition and manufacturing by Arcata Graphics.
Book design by Jacques Chazaud.

First Edition

Library of Congress Cataloging-in-Publication Data

Martin, Jay.
   Who am I this time? : uncovering the fictive personality / Jay Martin.
      p.   cm.
Includes index.
   1. Personality.   2. Psychoanalysis and literature.   I. Title.
BF698.M334 1988
155.2—dc19                                                                87–18749

ISBN 0-393-02525-X

W. W. Norton & Company, Inc., 500 Fifth Avenue, New York, N.Y. 10110
W. W. Norton & Company Ltd., 37 Great Russell Street, London WC1B 3NU

1 2 3 4 5 6 7 8 9 0

For
Helen


*The poets and the prophecies are ours:*
*and these are with us as we turn, in turn,*
*the leaves of love that fill the Book of Change.*

# Contents

# Author's Note

When I was seventeen years old, my aim in life was to become a poet. Conrad Aiken, who read some of my poems, arranged for their publication and invited me to live with him in his summer house in Brewster, on Cape Cod. He became a second father to me. Aiken's acquaintance with writers was a large one. Allen Tate, say, would come for a lunch one day; the next, we might make the trip over to Edmund Wilson's Wellfleet house. A letter from Tom Eliot might appear in the mailbox. Naturally, my own literary ambitions grew by leaps and bounds.

But I also began to learn how interested Aiken was in psychoanalysis. Analysts dropped in at the house almost as often as writers did, and conversation touched on psychological subjects strange and intriguing to me. One day I heard the extraordinary news that Sigmund Freud had been so impressed by one of Aiken's books that he had offered him a free analysis which, in the end, Aiken had refused!

As my own career developed, the literary side of it unfolded first and I eventually passed from the writing of poems to criticism, literary history, biography, drama, and fiction.

Still, I never forgot the other side of Conrad's interests, the psychoanalytic side. Slightly over a decade ago I started psychoanalytic training, and in 1978 began practice as a psychoanalyst. Conrad Aiken's dual interests, which he passed on to me, led to this doubleness in my own life. But it was perhaps also the doubleness of our times that fused itself into my development.

The present book brings these strands together. It is about literary works and about real people who find their identities in literature—literature of all kinds: fairy tales, television shows, comic strips, novels, poems. I write about assassins, terrorists, authors, actors and actresses, psychoanalysts, an army general, my own patients and those of others. My focus shifts from individual instances to cultural phenomena; from celebrated to unknown people; from the productive use of fictions to their destructive consequences.

What I call "the fictive personality," however, is always at the center of my scrutiny. It will take the book that follows to tell fully what I mean by this concept, but I can make a start here. The fictive personality is the disease that so disturbed the man who became known as Don Quixote de la Mancha that he replaced his own personality with the fictions that he derived from extensive readings in the tales of chivalric romance. He lost or suspended his own unsatisfactory self and replaced it with the characters, thoughts, feelings, and actions created by others. Something splendid, as well as something frightening, happened to him as a result.

Identifications with fictions have occurred since the first time one man or woman told a story to another. Our modern pleasure in reading books or seeing spectacles has to do with trying out roles and trying on identities. In this book I discuss the way that normal personalities are defined by and normal identities realized through fictions, ranging from tales, fantasies, and wishes, to dreams of all sorts. Writers have always been aware of the importance of fictive processes, and we will see how Freud and his followers began to develop a theory of fictions in personality. In doing so, I myself write as a literary critic, a social investigator, and a psychoanalyst.

But fictive processes have another darker side. So I also investigate the ways in which fantasy and aggression can fuse in the personality and produce a world suffused with hostility, assassination, and terrorism. Social life today is certainly marked and marred by the eruption of fictions into violence.

Equally important, modern culture has become increasingly differentiated from traditional societies by the enormous enlargement of fictions through the fiction-producing qualities of the media. Newspapers, popular magazines, movies, and, most of all, television have so flooded modern culture with fictions that many people have difficulty distinguishing between social relations that are real and those that are fantasized. "Fictive culture" more accurately describes contemporary social life than do such phrases as "narcissistic," "minimalist," or "post-modern" culture; for the profusion of fictions is central to the creativity—and the crisis—of our modern condition.

From my reading I knew about fictive personality long before I was aware of what I knew. Not until I had to grapple with what my own patients began to tell me about the fundamental role of fictions in their lives did I see how central to life and self they were, and how much they were related to mental health and also mental illness, to social growth and social chaos. As my patients gathered the courage to tell me about their lives, I took the risk of learning to write this book. I have gone to school to my patients, even as they learned something in their work with me.

The cases that I discuss are highly disguised for the sake of confidentiality. I have occasionally asked former patients to allow me to touch upon specific aspects of their experiences with fictions; other cases I derived from discussions with colleagues and supervisees as well as from my reading of psychoanalytic reports. Still others are composites of several persons. No case is true in all its facts, and no one's privacy has been violated; but all the cases are true to life.

I cannot conclude this note without the pleasure of a number of acknowledgments. The book itself had its origin in an invitation from Richard Fox that I prepare lectures to deliver to a joint meeting of the Southern California and Los Angeles Psychoanalytic Societies. I was prompted to refine and develop my ideas by those who commented on my talks: Justin Call, Don DeFrancisco, James Grotstein, Winthrop Hopgood, Arthur Malin, and Robert Pynoos. Other colleagues and friends challenged me to go still further; these included: Roman Anshin, Louis Breger, Paul Click, Samuel Eisenstein, Eleanor Galenson, John Gedo, Ronald Gottesman, Albert Hutter, Peter Manning, George Pollock, and John Wright. Lena Pincus went out of her way to help me locate obscure articles. My daughter, Helen Taylor, helped me editorially in the book's final stages. For aid and inspiration of many kinds and many years' duration, I am grateful to Louis A. Gottschalk.

Arthur Farley invited me to speak on the topic at the Houston-Galveston Psychoanalytic Society: R. Gerald Fromm did the same at the Austen Riggs Center. When I spoke on the developmental aspects of the topic to the World Congress of Infant Psychiatry at Cannes, my colleagues on the same panel, Paulina Kernberg and Peter Giovacchini, gave me further encouragement and more to think about.

I spent a month at the Rockefeller Foundation's scholar's center at the Villa Serbelloni, reflecting and writing. A Senior Research Fellowship from the National Endowment for the Humanities allowed me to read widely and gave me the time to write. I have not yet exhausted the pleasure that I had in Bellagio or the profit I derived from the generosity of the NEH, and I expect to draw upon both for many years to come.

It is as simple to say as it is true that notwithstanding the plenitude of assistance acknowledged above, this book would never have been completed without the confidence and assistance of Carol Houck Smith. To her I owe a boundless debt.

Jay Martin
*Irvine, California*

Did Chouang dream he was a butterfly?
Or did the butterfly dream Chouang? If so,
why then all things can change, and change again,
the sea to brook, the brook to sea, and we
from man to butterfly; and back to man.
This 'I,' this moving 'I,' this focal 'I,'
which changes, when it dreams the butterfly,
into the thing it dreams of; liquid eye
in which the thing takes shape, but from within
as well as from without: this liquid 'I':
how many guises, and disguises, this
nimblest of actors takes, how many names
puts on and off, the costumes worn but once,
the player queen, the lover, or the dunce,
hero or poet, father or friend,
. . . . . . . . . . .
what's true in these, or false? Which is the 'I'
of 'I's'?

—CONRAD AIKEN, *A Letter from Li Po*

# Who
# Am I
# This Time?

# 1

# The Life You Live
# May Not Be Your Own

Harry Nash, the hero of Kurt Vonnegut's short story "Who Am I This Time?" is a clerk at a hardware store in North Crawford, Iowa. Painfully shy, he "wasn't married, didn't go out with women—didn't have any close men friends either. He stayed away from all kinds of gatherings because he never could think of anything to say or do. . . ." Somebody in the town once remarked, Vonnegut tells us, "that Harry ought to go to a psychiatrist." But the plain-speaking narrator of the story says, "I don't know what a psychiatrist could have turned up about him that the town didn't already know"; and, something of a psychoanalyst himself, the narrator adds that Harry's trouble was related to early abandonment: "he'd been left on the doorstep of the Unitarian Church when he was a baby, and he never did find out who his parents were."

The implication is that without the presence of real parents as a source of identification, Harry was not able to develop a "real" personality of his own. Instead, he had "fictive" parents, and he developed a personality derived from fictions.

The "gift" which accompanied Harry's colorlessness was acting ability. He was extraordinarily versatile, equally skillful at taking the parts, successively, of Henry VIII, Abe Lincoln, or Captain Queeg in *The Caine Mutiny Court-Martial*. Now the Mask and Wig Club has voted to do Tennessee William's *A Streetcar Named Desire* for the spring production. The director, who is also the story's narrator, asks Harry to take a part. "Who am I this time?" he asks, eager for a new identity. Harry is slated—naturally—for the Marlon Brando part, Stanley Kowalski. As soon as he picks up the playbook and starts reading, Harry is transformed and now seems "huge and handsome and conceited and cruel."

As the story unfolds, a colorless young woman named Helene comes to town to help install some new telephone company machines. She stays in any town for only eight weeks. She accurately describes herself as "a walking icebox." She confides to a woman in the town: "I don't want to be the way I am. . . . I just can't help it, living the way I've lived all my life. The only experiences I've had have been in crazy dreams of movie stars." She says she experiences life as if she is in a bottle. The narrator pretty much agrees. He remarks that "she had pretty blue eyes, but there sure wasn't much hope or curiosity in them." Still, he "got it in my head" that she might make a good Stella for the play. Stella was the wife of the Marlon Brando character, whom he wanted Harry Nash to play. Eventually, he brings Harry and Helene together.

"I wonder if you two would play the fight scene," the director says to Harry and Helene. " 'Sure,' said Harry, his eyes . . . on her. Those eyes burned up clothes faster than she could put them on. 'Sure,' he said, 'if Stella's game.' "

At first she seems listless, but soon she falls for Harry—or rather "Stanley"—like a ton of bricks as she plays this scene with him and really lives out the part as Stella, his wife. "When the scene was over, Helene Shaw was as hot as a hod carrier, as limp as an eel . . . she wasn't in any bottle any more. There wasn't any bottle to hold her up and keep her safe and clean. The bottle was gone."

The play goes well. Then, toward the end of rehearsals, one of the townspeople takes pity on Helene and explains: "Once the show's over—whatever you thought Harry was evaporates into thin air." She is shocked, but plans carefully.

Following the final performance, all the Marlon Brando in Harry disappears, and he starts to retreat into his invisible self. He tries to get away from the theater, but Helene seizes his hand and begs him to take her to the cast party. He refuses, but at least he agrees to open a present which she has brought him. This turns out to be a copy of *Romeo and Juliet*, with a ribbon marking the balcony scene. Helene induces Harry to read the dialogue with her. She points out Romeo's speech:

> Harry cleared his throat. He didn't want to read the line, but he had to. "With love's light wings did I o'er-perch these walls," he read out loud in his everyday voice. But then a change came over him. "For stony limits cannot hold love out," he read, and he straightened up, and eight years dropped away from him, and he was brave and gay. "And what love can do, that dares love attempt," he read. . . .

Gently, Helene leads Harry out of the theater as they continue to speak Shakespeare's lines.

In a week they are married. Later, Helene tells the narrator, "in the past week . . . I've been married to Othello, been loved by Faust, and been kidnapped by Paris." Would they be in the next production?—the narrator asks. "Who are we this time?" she wonders.

I do not know if Harry should have gone to a psychiatrist—after all, he did acquire a wife who seemed to know how to choose exciting parts—but I do know two things: that some of the Harrys encountered in this book do need treatment, while others share Harry's creative talent, and go so far beyond his capacity that their commitment to fictions invigorates their minds and frees them instead of confining them.

In Harry, Vonnegut created a character who is so simplified and so clear that he serves as an excellent introduction to the fictive personality. Almost anyone who reads the story will recognize elements of himself in Harry, even while perceiving that Harry's obsessive need for identification has something pathological about it.

To greater or less degree, we all identify with characters in the mass media, novels, plays, biographies, and with cultural stereotypes. Such identifications are largely normal; every person experiences them and learns from them. Our earliest experiences as infants consist of fictions about parents, not yet defined as parents even, but only as unnameable, unnamed "others." Later we identify with characters in stories, cartoons, film, or television.

What would life be *without* fictions? From these we build memory, character, perspectives upon the world, a life plan, what the psychoanalyst Ernst Kris calls "a personal myth," the manner in which we relate to others, and the modes by which we raise our own children. In this normal process of development, our identifications are likely to be multiple, diffuse, transient, conditioned, and highly qualified. No one fiction is likely to dominate our psychic lives or behavior, but all combine provisionally to shape our education.

At the other extreme, identification with fictions can become obsessive, monolithic, more or less permanent, unconditioned, and unqualified. People who experience themselves as empty may look to fictions to provide a fixed, predictable role to inform the personality in its internal self-representa-

tion and external behavior. Those who feel weak and ineffectual may find in fictions grandiose representations of power,
especially of power secretly possessed, as in the case of Clark
Kent, who becomes Superman, or Billy, who turns into
Captain Marvel. Fictions thus can provide a grandiose model
for the self which otherwise experiences itself as impotent.

Those who feel diffuse, fragmented, and unstable may
find rigid guidelines and premeditated shapes in fictions.
The empty self is filled with ready-made self-concepts; the
fragmented self is held together on the surface, producing
an illusion of real being. But all too often, beneath that lies
the reactive anger and depression that arose from early frustration and disappointment, when the budding self was left
helpless and unformed—in search first of parents; and, when
these failed, for other sources of new birth.

Fictions, then, can give rise to imagination and originality;
or, when fictions lead to imitation instead of invention, to
the birth of a negative element in the personality. When
the self cannot invent, it can too easily feel invented.

We all live as fictive persons some of the time. Sammler,
the hero of Saul Bellow's *Mr. Sammler's Planet*, was struck
by the visual aspects of this fact as he walked down Broadway
in New York City. There he found:

> All human types reproduced, the barbarian, redskin, or Fiji,
> the dandy, the buffalo hunter, the desperado, the queer, the
> sexual fantasist, the squaw, bluestocking, princess, poet, painter,
> prospector, troubadour, guerrilla, Che Guevara, the new
> Thomas à Becket. Not imitated are the businessman, the soldier,
> the priest, and the square. . . . They sought originality. They
> obviously were derivative. And of what—of Paiutes, of Fidel
> Castro? No, of Hollywood extras. Acting mythic. Casting them-
> selves into chaos, hoping to adhere to higher consciousness, to
> be washed up on the shores of truth.

As Sammler reflects upon the passing parade of people
who take on roles, he realizes that life without imitation is
impossible and unthinkable.

Better, thought Sammler, to accept the inevitability of imitation and then to imitate good things. The ancients had this right. Greatness without models? Inconceivable. One could not be the thing itself—reality. One must be satisfied with the symbols. Make it the object of imitation to reach and release the high qualities. Make peace therefore with intermediacy and representation. But choose higher representations. Otherwise the individual must be the failure he now sees and knows himself to be.

As Bellow suggests, the crucial difference for persons or cultures is not between being authentic and being fictive, but between growth-directing fictions and processes that misdirect growth and leave the individual and society frozen. The difference is between what Sammler calls "higher representations" and dead, brutal models that—inevitably—envelop the individual with their deadness and brutality.

Harry's character is a middling one—neither very creative nor especially harmful. In fictions, in the parts he played, he found a solution to his own sense of inauthenticity. His acting gave him relief from sorrow and emptiness, and it hurt no one. Fictions held him together.

Many of the people in this book are similar to Harry. They get along. A few, however, live at the margins of life. Some are creators in the extreme, others are killers.

We all identify with invented personalities, but we do not all need inventions to experience ourselves as persons. Harry is a fictive personality because he cannot live for himself: he exists only by adopting the fictions created by others.

It is a central fact of human life that each person invents a reality in which to live. We do not discover reality, we construct it. "Every man's world picture," Erwin Schrödinger writes in *Mind and Matter*, "is and always remains a construct of his mind and cannot be proved to have any other existence." We create our reality by the way we search for it and what we search for. But, of course, most of us assume that other people also exist and also have constructed for themselves truthful, useful versions of existence. So long as our construction of reality acknowledges that others are engaged in a process of invention similar to ours, the fact that we all invent is unlikely to cause a distortion in the personality, since in this case, other inventors are accorded reality of their own.

But because invention of life is necessary to the experiencing of life, some people become induced to feel a veil between themselves and the reality of others. They may not feel authentic unless they are playing parts. They may begin to experience only themselves as real while others seem invented. Or, they may suspect that everyone *else* is real, only they themselves lack reality. They feel as though in a dream. Roles beckon to them: *play me! live in me! become me!* Such sensations are heightened by novels, television, and other productions that offer magical experiences that are more intense than reality, and thus seem more real.

I realize that in writing about the fictive personality I will need to guard against seeing it everywhere, as if no other concept were needed to describe the whole of life. Yet, I am haunted by the sense that the world has become crowded with the fictive. And I suspect that my readers will also sense the presence of its spirit all around.

In this book I plan to explore the varieties of the fictive personality in individuals, in the arts, and in society, both in the past and in contemporary life. As my evidence develops, it will illuminate more and more clearly the nature and use—and distortions—of the fictive processes familiar to all of us. We'll see where they go right, and where, when they go wrong, they lead to destructiveness.

Clearly, I am seeking to demonstrate that an understanding of the influence of fictions in life can come from a variety of sources: from the daily news, from novels or plays, from patients, from biographical studies of creators and destroyers, from analysis of society, from case histories, and from investigation of the effects of media upon mental life and the behaviors it engenders. Sometimes I focus on points where evidence from art and society and clinical practice intersect, and where real patients, famous persons, and characters in books are studied side by side. Far from being confusing, this process will, I hope, show how writers have illuminated life, even as people have sought life in fictions.

In addition, it is particularly appropriate to look at fictive personality processes from a developmental angle. Particularly in early life, when self-confidence is shaken by trauma or when trust in others is shattered, a vacuum of attachment will result. At this point, early fantasy and fictions tend to rush to "fill in" the deficit; and the person will see himself through a preformed fiction, or see others through already created stories. The fictive personality originates when the self or the world seems inauthentic, fragmentary, or unavailable, so that only ready-made fictions seem whole and complete.

Woven into all of my explorations are accounts of real persons whose psychoanalyses help to sharpen our understanding of some aspects of the operations of fictions in persons. Patients provide special insights into the varieties of concerns I am exploring.

Finally, I enlarge my focus, moving from these various individual accounts into the study of fictions in culture. Here I am concerned with the important ways that fantasies are collectivized in media, especially television, as well as with the way that an individual's fiction can be projected into institutions. Today we are seeing a transformation in our understanding of culture; for the first time in the history of the world, culture is governed largely by fictions. Contemporary culture is "fictive culture."

What I am investigating, then, is not all of life, but it is of considerable importance in individual and collective life,

and essential for an understanding of the operations of personalities and society today. Without a knowledge of the fictive
personality, we are likely to become its victims.

I first became aware of the power of fictions as I sat in
my consulting room listening carefully to the associations
of my patients. There, relaxed in a comfortable chair, trying
to think along with someone else, my other life as a writer,
critic, and teacher of literature seemed far away. I suppose
I assumed then that "out there" I dealt with creativity and
fictions, while in the office I had a real person to deal with.
That was true—but not all the truth.

One morning a man in his early thirties began to teach
me the rest of the truth—that fictions can be the most real
parts of a personality. He began to talk about what he had
"wanted to be" when he was a child. His ambition, he said,
was to be an airplane pilot. He had come to that goal through
reading the comic strip "Terry and the Pirates." He said
that he had idolized the creator of the strip, Milt Caniff.
The influence exerted by the comic strip upon Terry, for
that was my patient's name as well, was so deep and long-
lasting that after high school graduation he had tried to enter
the Air Force Academy.

As I listened, I was also recalling that Terry was much
attracted to Oriental women. Did this have anything to do
with the early appeal for him of Terry's nemesis—the beautiful Dragon Lady? My patient Terry led an unadventurous
life. How had this come to pass, when an early identification
with the adventurer Terry suggested that he was fascinated
with romance? Or was it that his childhood had been strictly
regulated (as indeed it had been) and "Terry and the Pirates"
served as a compensation for the parental rules to which
he was obliged to submit? Terry often described himself
as "isolated," "frosty," "distant," and "spaced." Did these
derive from, or precede, his ambition to be an airplane pilot,

enclosed in his cockpit, alone, isolated in the sky; high above all others?

In truth, I made little headway at the time in answering any of these questions. But they started me thinking that if I could understand the fictions that were important to Terry—or anyone else—I could eventually build up a kind of archaeology of the self, excavating layer after layer of older narrative lives.

Meanwhile, now that I was able to hear Terry, I saw that he was telling me quite a lot about himself through his fictions. Three more comic-strip characters soon proved to have influenced him even more profoundly than "Terry and the Pirates." These were the Lone Ranger, Captain Marvel, and Superman. From the way he talked about them I could see they were somehow connected. I asked him about that.

"I used to identify strongly with them when I was a kid," he said. "Their identities always remained secret. From time to time they appeared—they exposed themselves, did good deeds, and disappeared again. They were strong and gentle, the personifications of good. I like that. I want to do good."

Certainly, they had appealed to him when he was a child because though each appeared to be weak, all three were really strong. For the weak and young man who becomes Captain Marvel when he pronounces the magic word "sha-zam!", or Clark Kent, who is transformed from a "mild-mannered" reporter to an aggressive fighter against crime, there is no connection between their "real" appearance and their "more real" inner identity. Even the Lone Ranger: he wears a mask and appears therefore to be an outlaw; but he does only good deeds. But more than that, each one of these figures concealed himself behind some mask of make-believe. Terry was still doing that. Did the fictions correspond to some childhood wish to hide, or did the fictions themselves help to encourage the submergence of his self into secrecy?

I could see that the influence of the Lone Ranger had gone deep. Terry met many people casually. He was careful not to reveal much of his self to anyone. But he consciously fantasized that after he left women they would wonder about him and yearn to be near him, but not even know where to find him. "Who *was* that masked man?" they would ask themselves. "They would never forget me and always think of me with longing, but they would never know anything about me." He could get close to his fictions, but they kept him from getting close to people. And now that he was an adult he imitated his early fictions in order to erect barriers between himself and others.

The trouble was, Terry had not used his experience of fictions in order to create a strong self through identification with good models. He had used his fictions to defend a weak self, to keep it safe from attack. Once we worked together to focus attention upon his early fictions, Terry's defenses dropped and he began to bring forward the factor that had prompted him to use fictions in the first place. He had identified with ready-made fictions because he feared most deeply that he had no identity of his own. He had to borrow theirs. He said:

"I see myself now as a patchwork collection of defenses, tricks. Illusions, with no dignity. Now, since the defenses are tumbling and we get nearer to me I get more and more concerned: there isn't a me. The sum total of me is in the illusions, and I'm afraid when we strip all these away, there won't be anything there. I'm just tricks and illusions. Maybe the fact I speak of 'I' means there is a me, but it's so small it's totally insignificant. I was born and my body grew, but I never did. I think that all my attempts—if I had any, and I *must* have had some—to develop were squelched, and I became convinced I was nothing and so I had to acquire pseudo-characteristics, costumes, whatever it was 'they' wanted from me. I found that out right in the beginning. But I couldn't please 'them' with the fakes either. I never satisfied—that's my essence. Anything to the contrary is an illusion, like a circus or a magic act, a play, 'make-believe.' So every new relation is a challenge to see how long I can confound them—showing images or reflections of things that don't exist. It's like I died when I was a child—but that's my secret. I came back to fool everybody. Everybody thinks I'm still there—but I do it with mirrors. How deep is a reflection?"

We soon saw that he was made of fictions: he seemed like a composite to himself. Trying to describe his inner helplessness, for instance, on one occasion he jumbled three stories together—of Anne Frank, Pinocchio, and Cinderella. "The real me," he said, "is just a frightened, hidden-away child like Anne Frank. I'm in a prison, forgotten, unnoticed. I am this little kid with a long nose because I've lied so long. I'm vulnerable, like a little girl in the corner among the ashes."

The great British child analyst D. W. Winnicott has shown that during childhood development a "false self" can get imbedded in the personality and become hard to get out. The whole life system is affected by the false self. Like a stream divided by a boulder, the subsequent experiences of life have to go around the false aspects built into the being. Terry's experiences had dropped some unyielding obstacles into his life's flow. He knew what had happened and what he had to do. "I'm feeling like I have to learn to be myself and not an invented person," he lamented.

Relatively early in treatment I heard about the fictions that had been inscribed into Terry's childhood personality. He had always been an omnivorous reader, and I also heard about his current reading. But I did not hear until a rather late stage any evidence that a crucial fiction had defined and fixed a part of his personality during adolescence.

Then one day when he was talking about the restlessness he frequently felt in his place of business, he said: "I felt that I had to get out. So I did. I went to the bookstore to buy a book, *Lord of the Rings*." Still, he couldn't go back to work. He drove without destination. He saw a prostitute walking the boulevard, and he stopped to talk to her, with "second thoughts the minute I did it." He drove on. Perhaps she would think about him after he drove away and wish that she could have gotten to know him.

The way he narrated the whole episode struck me as having an adolescent "style." He said that the whole thing was "a pile of shit," he felt like a phony, everything else was phony, he felt depressed. Then he came out explicitly with his fictive identification. It was with Holden Caulfield, hero of *The Catcher in the Rye*, one of the most famous novels of the last thirty years. "Last night," Terry said, after he went home, "I went to bed and slept for a couple of hours, then I awoke and lay there for about forty-five minutes. I got up and read *Catcher in the Rye*. I identify so closely with this kid. I feel exactly as Holden Caulfield feels. We both are completely alone." At this point, I decided that I would pick up on his assertion of "exact" or total identity between himself and Caulfield in order to see what needs compelled him to see himself "as if" he were Holden. I believe I now understood the point of view of his episode with the prostitute. I said, "Holden didn't fare any better with a prostitute." He acknowledged that it was so—he had "the same" feelings of disappointment and guilt that Holden had experienced. "I wonder if you see any reasons why else you identify with Holden?" I asked. Terry associated:

> "I see, I experience, the confusion in his mind and his desperation. He invites every cabby he meets to have a drink with him. Even a little girl in the park, a friend of his sister's, he invites to have a hot chocolate. First he goes one way, then another. The girl he asks to marry him he thinks is a royal pain in the ass anyway. He's so confused and frightened—I identify with that. I don't have any target, any direction. I don't seem to be effective at anything. This morning when I got up I felt I didn't want to come here—then five minutes

later I couldn't wait to come. I'm depressed but I'm not allowed to be."

"You won't allow yourself," I said.

"Look how Holden tried to do lots of things, some crazy things even, so he wouldn't have to feel depressed. His parents—just like mine—wouldn't allow him: mine wouldn't allow me, they didn't want to hear about it. I'd just like someone to give a damn about me."

I had heard his emphasis on Holden's parents' coldness as a distortion that he shares with Holden and also as Terry's projection of his own feelings into Holden, but I felt that the emotional focus was on his confusing depression and solitude, which is also Holden's problem; and so I said: "That's Holden's problem too."

"It seems to be. That's why I identify with him. Our situations are similar. He's been a failure at school and nobody gives a shit. He's trying hard not to give a shit too. I keep saying to myself, there's one big difference: Holden is sixteen and I'm thirty-two and I feel just like him. *He's* trying to find himself. He's trying to make some adjustment between himself and the world he doesn't understand, and he finds himself different from everyone. He wants so badly to fit in, and yet he can't find any place that's comfortable. I guess I'm saying that's *my* problem. What I see in the book is myself. We seem to be different from everyone else, incompatible. If I meet anybody who seems to slightly care to be sympathetic, I'll react just like Holden—I'll ask her to run away with me. I seem so much like Holden. I make myself like that. Holden is me. When I read *Catcher in the Rye*, and I've read it many times, I don't read it with an open mind: I put myself into it. It's not difficult. I see me in him."

"Holden is me"; "I am Holden." We can read it both ways.

Eventually, Terry was able to unblock the flow of his internal life. When his own identity seemed so tenuous, fictions had seemed to him to be his only way of preserving a self. Through his fictions we gained entry into his hidden self and got glimpses at his buried—but still influential—childhood and adolescent wishes and attitudes. By catching glimpses of his fictions, he started to perceive his real needs and he started to shape an adult identity.

Terry's identification with Holden Caulfield is particularly interesting because this character has had such a lasting influence on so many adolescents. *"The Catcher in the Rye,"* one recent critic has written, "is one of the sturdiest best-sellers of the post-World War II era—a staple of high-school English courses, and a standard according to which every newly published tale of tortured adolescence is inevitably judged." It seems likely that the longevity of its appeal is related to J. D. Salinger's capacity to catch and convey the adolescent's characteristic mixture of special, snobbish entitlement and insecurity.

This mixed appeal corresponded to Terry's own conflicts, but in him the identification with Caulfield remained relatively passive. As we shall see in the next chapter, however, in the identification with Holden there exists considerable potential for violence.

# 2

# Explosive Fictions

**P**iece by piece, from his childhood on, Mark David Chapman stitched together a crazy quilt of fictions—fragments, remnants, odds and ends—until at last he found two extraordinary identifications that brought all the rest together: first that he was privileged to become Holden Caulfield, and second, that in order to become Caulfield he had to kill that "phony," John Lennon.

As far back as Chapman could remember, he perceived the world in a very special way. He believed that everyone had the same experiences, and was puzzled and confused whenever he had intimations that this was not so. It seemed to him that his room was populated by a swarming mass of tiny people. "His childhood room," it was later said, "became his whole terrestrial globe; and he populated its walls with thousands of tiny people." Sometimes he realized that these tiny beings were not in the room, but rather inside his head, and that he only projected them into the room, which corresponded to his head. Occasionally he realized that these swarming people were concretions of his tumultuous thoughts, but since they did not usually seem to be his, but instead separate from him and even pushed into him, he tended to see them as possessing power and an existence separate from his own. Yet he did feel that the "little people" recognized his own supremacy over them. "I had control over their lives," he said; "they'd worship me like a king." He ruled over them, and they came to his aid whenever he needed it. For instance, when he had a decision to make, he would submit it to the council of the little people. They would discuss it with him and take notes and then their representatives would inform him of their decisions. When Mark was particularly troubled, he would call upon these tiny people and they would organize so as to defend him against his enemies.

Not all of the people swirling inside him had good characters, however; some of them were Satan's demons and they tried to fool him into adopting their evil purposes or bad thoughts. So he had to be careful about soliciting the help or advice of the inner multitudes. He later confessed that he could feel the presence of Satan's demons around him. . . . "I can feel their thoughts, I hear their thoughts. I can hear them talking, but not from the outside, from the inside."

Mark Chapman was an emperor of this self-created, projective world. But as he understood it, his power over it was qualified; the people were always forming new political parties, electing new representatives, and shifting old allegiances. All of this was confusing and unsettling, since it became so hard to tell which advice was phony or was even maliciously calculated to do him harm. In *Crime and Punishment* Fyodor Dostoevski showed a dramatically clear understanding of the sort of schizophrenic process which Chapman experienced. Dostoevski allows his hero Raskolnikov to explain that he had had a dream that showed him the source of his delusions: a swarm of microbes had gotten inside his head. The analyst Edward Glover has described this mental state very well in his theory of ego nuclei. The ego, he explains, is formed of various fragments that are combined to form a unified whole by early developmental processes of integration. But if they remain nuclei, the self experiences itself from outside, and these fragments seem to be autonomous and to lead a separate existence inside one's personality.

According to Murray Kempton's summary of testimony at the trial, Chapman's inner and outer lives were sharply divided. Chapman was born in Fort Worth, Texas, but grew up in Atlanta, Georgia. For as long as anyone could remember, despite his own fantasy that he was the emperor of a vast internal empire, he appeared to others to be searching for something to believe in and someone to obey. His whole life seems to have been based upon the drive toward finding himself in others. Around the age of fifteen he had an intense religious experience. "He felt like the Lord had touched him, that he had turned his life around. He wanted to prove that he was a good person, that there was no bad person inside of him."

"God" alone did not satisfy Chapman's hunger for good feelings inside him, for good relations, for love, or for admiration. He sought these from everyone he met. Tony Adams, the director of the De Kalb, Illinois, YMCA where Mark worked and formed his first plan for a career as a YMCA worker, said that he "would do anything to please me." The girl he was passionately devoted to, a self-assured young woman named Jessica, provided him with what he regarded as a fully formed set of values: he joined her religion and became fully persuaded of its perfection; he dressed and ate and drank as she did; he imitated her nonviolence; he went to the college she recommended. According to one of

Mark's closest friends, "virtually everything [he] did during that period he did because of Jessica. His whole involvement with religion. Even what he ate and drank. He wouldn't drink alcohol, or Coca-Cola, or any kind of soda pop—anything that was bad for your body. He said how displeased she would be if he had a beer. He was so concerned with doing the Christian-like thing."

It seems clear that Chapman intensely experienced the divisions within him, and explained them to himself as the warfare inside his soul of good and bad spirits. Needing someone—anyone—to follow, he followed the bad spirits as enthusiastically as he followed the good ones. At the same time that he was imitating Jessica and attempting to lead an exemplary life, he had been influenced by other friends to take drugs—"he did anything he could get his hands on," one friend said. Jessica was a pacifist, but David also idealized another friend who toted a pearl-handled revolver, and he later took pistol training and became a security guard. No wonder he said that he was fighting with "good and evil spirits." His life started to fall apart. He dropped out of college. Jessica broke off with him. He decided to go to Honolulu—it seemed to him to be part of a secret destiny to do so.

The conviction that he had a special destiny to fulfill was, of course, a probable sign of schizophrenia. In Hawaii, Chapman's thinking became so confused that he was admitted for psychiatric care at Castle Memorial Hospital in Honolulu. After a brief treatment he was discharged. Later, he applied for an orderly's job in the same hospital and was hired. He performed satisfactorily in attending to elderly patients, but he seemed obsessed with the subject of firearms.

He must have been tormented internally by his conflicts. He wanted to do good and be good, to be on the side of his "good spirits." But he had not been able to stay in college or win his girl friend. Instead, he seemed to be gliding onto the side of his "bad spirits." He made an ineffective suicide attempt, but death—his own death—wasn't the answer. Although he failed to kill himself, he said, "My life is gone," anyway. On September 10, 1980, he wrote a letter to a friend; it said, "I'm going nuts." It was signed, "The Catcher in the Rye. . . ." He even wrote to the office of the attorney general of Hawaii inquiring about changing his name to "Holden Caulfield."

Shortly thereafter Chapman travelled to New York City. His plan—*Holden's* plan—was forming in his head. He told himself that he was destined to become a famous person. He catapulted himself into the news by murdering John Lennon of the Beatles outside the Dakota, the apartment building where Lennon lived. He pumped five slugs from a .38-caliber Charter Arms revolver into Lennon. Then, immediately following the shooting, Chapman calmly removed his coat and sweater—apparently so that the police, when they arrived, would see that he was unarmed and intended no further harm—and took his copy of *The Catcher in the Rye* out of his pocket and read with intense concentration.

In Chapman, extreme confusion about his self fused with an array of "good" and "bad" identifications. Further evidence of this confusion showed up in his obsession with Norman Rockwell's painting *Triple Self-Portrait*, where Rockwell looks into a mirror as he paints his reflection on a canvas. This was Chapman's central problem: Where is the "I"? Is it in the fictive, painted, observer artist; the fictive mirror; or the fictive art? There seemed no other alternatives. *Everything* was a fiction.

Out of this confusion Chapman had begun to identify with John Lennon. He played the guitar, he collected Beatles records, he married a Japanese-American woman as did Lennon; she helped to support him. When he quit his last job six weeks before the murder he signed his final worksheet with the name "John Lennon." He hung around the Dakota. He told a taxi driver who picked him up in front of the apartment that he had just dropped off the tapes of a new album that Lennon and Paul McCartney had made that day. On the day of the murder, he approached Lennon to auto-graph his latest album, *Double Fantasy*, and he made certain that a photographer snapped his picture with Lennon. He urged the photographer to remain on the scene until Lennon returned. "You never know," he said, "something might happen." The photographer left, but Lennon came back. Chapman still had Lennon's autographed album with him when he shot the singer.

Based on psychiatrist Daniel Schwartz's testimony at the sentencing, we can say with fair certainty what had hap-pened. Having failed to kill himself, Chapman's identification with Lennon became more and more sinister. He projected his own suicidal wishes onto the object of his identification. Then, to kill the bad things in himself, he had only to kill his double, Lennon. Recently, he had come to consider Len-non a "phony," a betrayer of his generation's ideals, an im-poster. To kill Lennon would be to kill his own "bad" side.

Apparently Chapman came to see his task as the purifica-tion of his fictions. If he could kill the phony, "bad" Lennon— "a forty-year-old businessman who watches a lot of television, who's got $150 million, a son whom he dotes on, and wife who intercepts his phone calls"—then Satan's demons would be defeated and as a result the world, and Chapman himself, would be cleansed. One last time, he called the "cabinet" of his internal world into session and submitted to the little people the proposal that he kill the John Lennon imposter. In that event, the real Lennon would become, once more, "the emblem and conscience of an age," which is to say, he would fuse with Holden Caulfield, and these would suffuse the internal being of Mark David Chapman. He would be-come Lennon-Caulfield.

During the initial hearings, when asked why he had killed Lennon, Chapman often remarked, in what he seemed to think was an answer, that the meaning was to be found in Salinger's book. He was, he said, the "Catcher in the Rye" for his generation, and he talked at length about the innumerable, complicated similarities that he saw between himself and Holden Caulfield during Holden's three days in New York, which provide the substance of the novel. *The Catcher in the Rye* was certainly a work peculiarly suited to "containing" Chapman's fragments. Holden, in the book, is obsessed with loss and death. After his brother Allie dies, the whole world seems phony to him, except for his sister Phoebe. His parents drop out of his consciousness, and he is left alone to mourn the loss of his brother, and to make up for his death by doing good in the world.

Chapman told Daniel Schwartz, who prepared material for the defense, that earlier on the day of the shooting he believed that immediately upon killing Lennon he would turn into Caulfield and cease to exist in his own identity. It seems, at least in part, that he really believed this to have happened, since at his sentencing in late August 1981, he told Judge Dennis Edwards, Jr., that he had only a few words to say before he would begin a vow of silence. But when he spoke, his words came directly from Salinger's novel—only Chapman recited them as if they were his own words and as if they expressed the precise position at which he personally had arrived.

> I kept picturing all these little kids playing some game in this big field of rye and all. Thousands of little kids, and nobody's around—nobody big, I mean—except me. And I'm standing on the edge of some crazy cliff. What I have to do, I have to catch everybody if they start to go over the cliff—I mean if they're running and they don't look where they're going I have to come out from somewhere and catch them. That's all I'd do all day. I'd just be the catcher in the rye and all. I know it's crazy, but that's the only thing I'd really like to be.

"You and I," Daniel Schwartz told the judge, "try to model ourselves after somebody . . . we will not run the risk of believing that we are that person." But Chapman did. Eventually he projected his own hatred and inward sense of phoniness onto Lennon, so that he could view himself as pure and honest. Now, pure, he spoke directly to God. Eventually God told him to plead guilty and allowed him to become Holden Caulfield, and to speak Holden's words. He *had* killed phoniness, he *had* murdered evil, he *had* rid the world of death: he *was* the catcher in the rye. Chapman's final testimony amounted to this—that he himself had ceased to exist. In a letter to his wife he stated that this was so— he no longer existed in his own being. He had wholly become his good fiction; he had found his true being in Salinger's novel.

Reactions to Lennon's death were immediate. The funeral service in Central Park was an unmitigated main event. Ten minutes of planned silence were concluded by a great un-planned outburst of applause—the members of the audience saw themselves as participants in an "event," and, as if this were a theatrical spectacle rather than a memorial, they spon-taneously applauded themselves. The event was covered by a major network and reviewed in *The New York Times* by that paper's theater critic, Frank Rich, and its book reviewer, John Leonard. A thirty-year-old man in Utah and a teen-age girl in Florida committed suicide, leaving notes saying that the cause was Lennon's death.

Among the mourners was a young man named John Hinck-ley, who travelled to New York "in deep mourning" specifi-cally to join the Lennon vigil in Central Park. A few weeks after this ceremony, this same young man confided to his tape recorder: "I just want to say good-bye to the old year, which was nothing, total misery, total death. John Lennon is dead, the world is over, forget it." Many months later, after he had attempted to assassinate President Reagan,

Hinckley responded to a question about whom he admired—showing, in the process of doing so, both the nature of his identifications and also a remarkable lack of a sense of contradiction: "I don't admire any political leaders, except perhaps Mr. Reagan. The only person I ever idolized . . . was John Lennon, and look what happened to him."

How did this devotee of John Lennon and admirer of President Reagan arrive at a Washington, D.C., Hilton hotel entrance, fingering his revolver, waiting for the president to step from the door to his limousine? Without a doubt he arrived there armed not only with a pistol but with a core set of fictive identifications that led him to believe that he was on stage at a magnificent theatrical spectacle.

The most remarkable thing about Hinckley's childhood was its blank normality. The third of three children, he apparently felt that he had little chance of measuring up to his older brother, who graduated from Vanderbilt University as an engineer and joined his father's oil exploration business; or to his sister, who was a high-school favorite (head cheerleader, homecoming-queen candidate, vice-president of the choir, and a member of the A-students' National Honor Society) while John went to the same school in her shadow. He was always in the shadows: "John was mousy," a school acquaintance said, ". . . John never did anything outstanding or memorable." Another classmate remarked that he was "so normal he appeared to fade into the woodwork." There was even a sad ironic note in his father's response when told that an attempt had been made on the president's life—an action that was, after all, anything but unremarkable—and that the suspect carried papers with the name John W. Hinckley, Jr. "It had to be a stolen ID," John, Sr., said in disbelief. Here was, truly, a young man who seemed to lack all qualities.

In contrast to Chapman, who apparently experienced his inner world with a cast of thousands, Hinckley seems to

have had an empty, schizoid interior life, which started slowly
to fill up with fictions. It is impossible to say when these
started. As a student at Texas Tech, he did little work.
His landlord says that "he just sat there the whole time,
staring at the TV." One class, at least, did spark some interest
in him—German history, for which he wrote papers on *Mein
Kampf* and Auschwitz. Something about these took hold,
and two years later he became a member of the National
Socialist Party of America and marched in a Nazi parade
in St. Louis. He urged his comrades to begin to shoot people
in order to further their programs, and was purged from
the party's membership in 1979. He published a newsletter
for a supremacist party of his own design, the "American
Front," which he designated "a viable alternative to the mi-
nority-kissing Republican and Democrat's parties," a party
"for the proud White conservative who would rather wear
coats and ties instead of swastikas and sheets." He conferred
the grandiose title "National Director" upon himself and
invented a list of members from thirty-seven states. The
organization, of course, was thoroughly fictive—though
hardly original. It was a fiction based on the old Nazi fictions.

On his own he began to collect a small arsenal and to
carry guns with him. By the fall of 1980, he had begun to
live in a special sort of fictive drama: he hunted and stalked
President Jimmy Carter during the presidential campaign.
In October, he travelled to Nashville where President Carter
was making a campaign appearance. At the Nashville airport
Hinckley was arrested for attempting to board a New York
flight carrying hand luggage that contained three revolvers
and fifty rounds of ammunition. He was promptly released
after posting a fifty-dollar bond, and the FBI was not
informed of his arrest. Yet, as films later indicated, he
was also in the crowd in Dayton, Ohio, that greeted Carter as he stepped from his limousine to the convention center.

The source of Hinckley's actions emerged with stark clarity. But no one had any reason to notice. He had begun to live in a movie, *Taxi Driver*, directed by Martin Scorsese, and to identify almost totally with the main character of that movie, Travis Bickle, played by Robert De Niro.

To understand the fictive person whom John Hinckley had become it is necessary to consider the psychological appeals of the film. In *Taxi Driver*, the camera is used expressionistically, so that the viewer is trapped inside it, and confined to the emotions it conveys. We see only what the camera sees and are held rigidly to its point of view. No "reality" can be inferred outside the angle of the camera's vision. In turn, the camera's perspective, we come to see, is organized according to the disturbed psyche of the main character, Travis Bickle, so that the viewer is caught within an agonized vision: what the camera sees, and the perspectives and angles and distortions of its seeing, gives us, with great immediacy, the way that Bickle understands the world.

Bickle's vision of New York City is distinctively his own—a very limited, perverted vision. The viewer has to get outside the film, by reading Alfred Kazin or Isaac Bashevis Singer on New York, or watching Woody Allen's *Hannah and Her Sisters*, to realize that Bickle understands the city solely as a place of corruption, filth, violence, dread—an open sewer, filled with garbage and inhabited by human vermin. Only pimps and pushers and prostitutes walk the streets; only whores and their johns ride in cabs; only slime flows; it is a city of dreadful night and the night's creatures.

The opening sequence shows how Bickle's mind works and how the camera functions to confine the viewer. In general, the style of the film is to stress explosive instants rather than narrative flow, since Bickle's fragmentary internal life sees the world in incandescent moments. The first sight we get is of a fragment: part of a taxi-cab, the front end, emerges ominously from steam coming from the sewer-underworld, an underground hell that the film implies is always operating in Bickle's fetid but puritanical, rule-ridden unconscious. The camera jumps from its focus on part of a car to focus on part of a person: it fixes on Travis Bickle's eyes; in the neon lights, his eyes seem ablaze with a red glare, then they become normal, then red again. The music becomes noticeable. Bernard Herrmann's dissonant, nervous, percussive score encourages a feeling of psychological disorientation and ominous fears; like the camera, broken into fragments, the music models our emotions. Travis's eyes move back and forth; we see that we are only seeing reflections of his eyes in his cab's rear-view mirror, not the eyes themselves.

Then we are pushed behind his eyes inside his head. We see what he sees along with his perceptual distortions: people are hard-edged, they move in slow motion, they leave trails of light, tinted blue and red, hidden in smoke. The audience is thrust inside Travis' thoughts. We hear his words: "All the animals come out at night—whores, skunk-pussies, beggars, queens, fairies, dopers, junkies. . . ." That is all he can see: his view of reality is one-dimensional, and the viewer—especially any viewer with a weakened sense of reality—is twisted and molded by the perceptual process of the film into a more and more narrow understanding of the world.

As the camera follows Travis around, it sees Travis's perceptions: scenes of anger, antagonism, suspicion. The way that it keeps going off center, pushing Travis to the periphery of the frames and sometimes even dropping him out of the frame entirely, exhibits his own out-of-focus world, and shows how far he is disoriented in his understanding of himself, as well as of objects. He is alone, cut off, unable to relate to anyone. Ultimately, the film gets nowhere; the movie ends where it starts. Peter Boyle, one of the actors, has said that the performers agreed "that what happens in the film is that Travis ends up exactly where he was at the beginning." Again, he is looking in the rear-view mirror. People move in slow motion. He is alone, still trapped in himself, unchanged. Everything about the film is enclosed and enclosing. Confined spaces, narrow hallways, one-way streets, cluttered rooms—these and other images well convey the claustrophobia of Travis's aloneness; he even talks to himself.

But between the beginning and the end lies the illusion of activity. Increasingly pressured by his own painful inner reality and the way that, through his projections, "reality" seems to confirm his fears and suspicions and angers, Bickle purchases several guns. After he fails to make a successful romantic relationship with Betsy, a political-campaign worker, he goes into personal paramilitary training in the mode of a tactical forces specialist with the intent of assassinating the political candidate for whom she worked. He shaves his head into a Mohawk-style cut and approaches the candidate at a political rally, only to be spotted and chased by an FBI agent. He escapes, and then decides that his real object should be to "save" a young prostitute, Iris, played by Jodie Foster, from her pimp. He does kill the pimp, as well as two others, while he is shot and stabbed in a bloody finale. At the end he makes the same gesture he has made before—pointing his first finger as if it were a gun at his head, he brings his thumb down like a cocked hammer, playing at shooting himself. But his playing has been real: all along he has been living in fictions that express his death-wish.

However, he does not die. He is brought to a hospital, is treated, and recovers. Some time passes, and the film finds him back in his room. He has become a media hero. His walls are plastered with clippings about his role in "freeing" the underage girl from prostitution; in the course of his efforts he has killed a member of the Mafia. He has found his identity: it comes from the newspaper articles

about him. All along, Travis has been seeking suitable fictions
to play out. Mostly his fictions come from the *New York
Daily News*, television programs, porno films, and such movies
as those that appear on the marquees beneath which he walks:
*Death Wish*, *Seven Blows of the Dragon*, *The Mafia Wanted Blood*,
and *The Texas Chain-Saw Massacre*.

Bickle's wish to kill a political candidate—one, moreover,
whom he professes to admire—clearly has as its background
the notoriety received by Lee Harvey Oswald. His aim to
free Iris from her pimp is a distortion of the film *The Searchers*,
in which John Wayne seeks to free a young white woman
who has been captured by Indians. In his haircut, he identifies
with Uncas in *The Last of the Mohicans*. With Betsy, he attempts
to play a Cary Grant-type role; later, he imitates Brando
in *On the Waterfront*, James Dean, and sometimes Woody
Allen. He speaks lines which he has palpably learned from
the movies; "I might be going away for a while," he whispers
to Iris. Betsy compares his character to a fictional person
in a song: "He's a prophet and a pusher, partly truth, partly
fiction, a walking contradiction."

The scriptwriter of *Taxi Driver*, Paul Schrader, has said
that he built Travis's character from the story of Arthur
Bremer, who attempted to kill George Wallace. Himself
an evident example of a fictive personality, Bremer fantasized
for himself a special version of what Freud called the "Family
Romance": he liked to think that his "true" mother was the
actress Donna Reed—but Donna Reed of "The Donna Reed
Show," not the "real" person. Bremer said that he was inspired by the movie *A Clockwork Orange* to carry out his
attempt on the life of Wallace, who was, at that time, in
contention for the Democratic presidential nomination. After
the shooting, Bremer was quoted as expressing satisfaction:
"Well, I was on Cronkite's program today," he boasted.

No wonder that Travis Bickle took hold of John Hinckley's
imagination: from the screen one palpably fictive personality

called to another. As Hinckley flatly said in one of his "poems," titled "Prince Valium," "fantasies become reality in my world." In the same tape recording in which Hinckley commented about John Lennon's death, he added: "Anything I do in 1981 will be totally for Jodie Foster's sake." He had already written a highly theatrical anonymous letter to the FBI: "There is a plot underway to abduct actress Jodie Foster from a Yale University dorm in December or January. No ransom. She's being taken for romantic reasons."

In the clearest possible way, Hinckley was living the plot of Travis's film and incorporating Travis's personality into his own. He bought an army fatigue jacket, army boots, and plaid shirts, just like those worn by Travis. He drank peach brandy, as Travis did; he bought three guns because Travis bought three (one of them was a Charter Arms .38 because that was the weapon used to kill John Lennon). Travis took over-the-counter pills: Hinckley began to take Tylenol, Drixoral, Surmontil, and Valium. He kept a diary, just as Travis had done. He invented a girl friend for himself, whom he named Lynn Collins, and who resembled Betsy. He behaved exactly like a "copycat" killer, except that he was copying a palpable fiction. (Copycat killers actually do that too, since all they know of their model is derived from the media.) He was thoroughly obsessed with his aim of freeing Jodie Foster from Yale where she was (as he saw it) imprisoned. Agents who searched his room after the attempted assassination found an unmailed letter to Ms. Foster in which he promised to command her attention for the "historic deed" he was about to commit. By killing the president, he believed, he would become united with her. He did in fact tell *Newsweek* that before the assassination attempt she intimidated him, but "now I think we are equal and rather compatible. Don't you agree?" When she said on a videotape played during the trial that she had no relations with him, he ran out the courtroom. He could only face fiction. Still, after the shooting Hinckley wrote to *Newsweek:* "Travis keeps telling Jodie that he wants to help her escape all of these sordid characters that are ruining her, but she doesn't understand what he is talking about and resists him. I know exactly how Travis felt."

Eventually, Hinckley's goals in life narrowed down to two: to kill a political figure and to win Jodie Foster's love by liberating her. He was ready to kill any political figure, it seems: anyone would do. Following the election, he lost interest in former President Carter. Then he planned to kill Senator Edward Kennedy and actually went to his Washington, D.C., office. He brought his Charter Arms .38 pistol with him. It was important that the gun be the same kind that had killed Lennon; somehow that would make up for the singer's death. He wrote a poem or song titled "Guns Are Fun," which conveys something about his state of mind:

> See that living legend over there?
> With one little squeeze of this trigger
> I can put that person at my feet
> moaning and groaning and pleading with God.
>
> This gun gives me pornographic power.
> If I wish, the president will fall!
> and the world will look at me in disbelief,
> all because I own an inexpensive gun.
>
> Guns are loveable. Guns are fun
> Are you lucky enough to own one?

Eventually, he did find an opportunity to shoot President Reagan, himself a former actor and media personality, of course. During the shooting, psychiatrist William T. Carpenter testified, Hinckley felt as if he were "just there, living out an experience," in which the participants "were bit players."

Certainly, Hinckley, in his own approach to the event,

suggested that he was not acting on his own, but in a scenario. When *Newsweek* asked him about all the guns in his possession, he said that he personally was in favor of gun control, but "I bought so many handguns because Travis bought so many handguns. Ask him, not me." Hinckley said of Bickle: "If there was more people like that Robert De Niro played in the movie . . . there wouldn't be any problem controlling crime." He believed that the showing of Ms. Foster's films on TV were meant as a secret message to him.

Like someone collecting scrapbooks, Hinckley seems to have collected a variety of fragmentary identifications to support his central one with Bickle. In room 312 of the Park Central Hotel, he prepared for the shooting by assembling photographs of Lee Harvey Oswald and a color calendar and song lyrics by Lennon; he penned a note about his resemblance to Hitler—"an unimportant, common person who rose to eminence," he noted—and Charles Whitman, who went on a shooting spree at the University of Texas, Austin, in 1966.

He had several books. One, Nathaniel Benchley's *Welcome to Xanadu*, clearly corresponds to his fantasies about Jodie Foster; it tells the story of a patient who escapes from a mental hospital, then kidnaps a woman and takes her to an isolated cabin where he wins her love; when the police arrive he kills himself. Another, Bob Randall's *The Fan*, is about a man who pursues a screen star and eventually kills her, then himself. A third was Eliot Asinof's *The Fox Is Crazy Too*, a journalistic account of Garrett Trapnell, who hijacked a plane; at his trial, although it was evident that he was mentally ill, he also deliberately "pretended" to be insane. From the words of the hijack note used by Trapnell, Hinckley made a hijack note of his own, and this too was found in his room, inserted into a Band-Aid box, ready to hand to a flight attendant. Among other papers found in his room were a postcard of Ronald and Nancy Reagan with a message to Jodie Foster: "Don't they make a darling couple? Nancy is downright sexy. One day you and I will occupy the White House and the peasants will drool with envy. Until then, please do your best to remain a virgin." He also had a picture of Napoleon and Josephine that he had labeled "John and Jodie." And last, out of fictive identification with Mark David Chapman, he bought a copy of *The Catcher in the Rye*.

In short, John Hinckley had become little more than a scrapbook, the composite of his fictions. He had some awareness of this, for when the editors of *Newsweek* asked him whether books and movies influence the way people behave "in real life," he replied enthusiastically: "Yes, Yes, Yes. The line dividing Life and Art can be invisible." After seeing "enough hypnotizing movies and reading enough magical books," he added, "a fantasy life develops which can be . . . quite dangerous." Asked about the influence of television and the ability of the medium to convey "what's going on in the world" accurately, Hinckley responded with some indignation: "Watching too much television can cause numerous social disorders." Yet, from this reasonable awareness was split off an independently operating fictive personality. It was this personality that prepared a speech he intended to read when he received an expected guilty verdict: "God does indeed work in mysterious ways. My life has become a melodrama. . . . I am now a household name."

He was right. Declared not guilty by reason of insanity and remanded to St. Elizabeth's Hospital in Washington, D.C., when he arrived at the hospital, he found that he was in demand. A large number of workers there approached him for autographs. For all intents and purposes, he had achieved the destiny of his hero Travis.

Travis Bickle's effect upon John Hinckley was, of course, enormous. But Hinckley was not alone in feeling the power of *Taxi Driver*. Martin Scorsese's film brings together in an extraordinary way the secret fantasies of many people to achieve identity by getting close to prominent people—sometimes by killing them, sometimes through less violent means. *Taxi Driver* is not the only film in which Scorsese deals with this subject matter. A movie title *The King of Comedy*, which appeared a few years after *Taxi Driver*, has a similar theme. In the film, Rupert Pupkin envies the host of a talk show, modeled on Johnny Carson, and aspires to replace him on the show. Though he has had no professional experience, Pupkin believes that he is "star material." In his house in Clifton, New Jersey, he has constructed a stage set in which he *is* the talk-show host. Here he interviews pasteboard "people" like "Jerry Langford" (the Johnny Carson figure) and Liza Minelli. He plays a laugh-and-applause sound effects record that gives the "reactions" of a pasteboard "audience." His room is filled with stacks of comic books, books on comedy, and posters of comedy stars. He is the sort of person who lives so completely in his fictions that when he pulls out his autograph book to impress a young woman on a date, his own signature is smack in the middle, between those of Marilyn Monroe and Mel Brooks. He manages to get into talk-show host Langford's car as he leaves the show, and has a brief conversation with him that leads to many fantasies that he will become a guest on Jerry's show and later replace him as the host, just as "Jerry" had replaced Jack Paar. "It's the obsession of wanting something so strongly," Scorsese said in an interview, ". . . that you take it to the point of acting out fantasies."

Rupert identifies with Jerry so completely that he decides to kidnap him and, as a condition for Jerry's release, replace him on the show. His demand for air-time is actually granted, and he delivers a comic monologue based on the misery of his life, his parents' alcoholism, his own continuous vomiting, the beatings his parent gave him, and so on. "Better to be king for a night than schmuck for a lifetime," he concludes. The monologue is a brilliant one. At its conclusion Pupkin willingly goes off to jail on kidnapping charges, but he receives tremendous publicity for his bizarre feat. His monologue has been seen by eighty-seven million American households, he is put on the cover of *People* magazine, and *King for a Night*, the tragi-comic autobiography that he writes in jail, sells over one million copies. As soon as he is released he is invited to appear on television. The announcer introduces him: "TV's biggest new star, the legendary, inspirational, one and only king of comedy, Rupert Pupkin!"

Does this success in the aftermath of the kidnapping actually occur or is it only in Rupert's mind? The movie does not allow the viewer to know: the point is that, in either case, fictions and reality have become so confused that reality is fictional and fictions are real, in both personality and contemporary culture.

Paul Zimmerman, the scriptwriter of *The King of Comedy*, explained its origin in an interview in *American Film*: "In 1970, I saw a David Susskind show on autograph hunters, and thought, 'My God, they're just like assassins.' I also read a piece in *Esquire* about a guy who kept a diary of talk-show hosts as though they were his friends. I began to imagine the possibility of one of these fringe people developing in his head a personal relationship with a television personality, and then getting together somehow."

From years of watching Langford on television, along with reading every scrap available about him, Rupert believes that he really knows the talk-show host, and even vaguely feels that Jerry may owe him some gratitude for being such a faithful follower. Rupert's character was played so convincingly by Robert De Niro that some reviewers thought the movie might lead to copy-cat kidnappings of talk-show hosts. Indeed, it was reported that Johnny Carson had turned down the Jerry Lewis-Jerry Langford part, fearing it would invite imitators of Pupkin to attempt a similar kidnapping. It was this fear that caused movie columnist Marilyn Beck to call the picture "the most irresponsible film . . . since *Taxi Driver*, and . . . potentially more dangerous." Scorsese himself confessed to being personally frightened in March 1983 when, as he was editing *The King of Comedy*, Teresa Saldana, an actress who had played in one of his earlier films, *Raging Bull*, was stabbed four times in front of her West Hollywood apartment by a man who knew her only from her appearances on screen. For months Scorsese seldom went out, and he became protective about the people who worked for him, calling them up and advising them to be careful. His most recent film, *The Color of Money*, is quite different from *Taxi Driver* and *The King of Comedy*, suggesting that he had scared even himself with the fictions he produced.

Each in his own way, J. D. Salinger and Martin Scorsese were able to create or give vivid life to characters that arouse deep, primitive reverberations in many people, and foster the development of murderous fantasies in sick, schizoid people. As heroes from *The Iliad* made a constellation of myth and belief for ancient Greeks, Salinger and Scorsese's "heroes" provide very central myths for our times, but they confirm not so much our beliefs as our fears.

# 3

# The Jackal
# and Terrorism

"What a glorious opportunity for a man to immortalize himself by killing Abraham Lincoln!" John Wilkes Booth exclaimed two years before committing that very crime. In planning the assassination, he insisted that Lincoln should be killed in a theater, where Booth could jump upon the stage shouting *Sic semper tyrannis*, just as Brutus had done when Julius Caesar was killed. For him, long before Chapman and Hinckley, assassination was performance. Other contemporary killers have frequently expressed the idea that fame was the motive that spurred them on. "They can gas me, but I am famous," exulted Sirhan Sirhan. "I have achieved in one day what it took Robert Kennedy all his life to do." From Booth to Sirhan, terrorists and assassins have murdered as a way of seizing their victims' lives and turning them into identities of their own. And the process is very evident in numerous more recent terrorist activities.

In Vienna, for instance, in December 1975, a young, heavyset man scans a group of powerful OPEC oil ministers with his automatic pistol. He wears a Basque beret, below which flows long, curly hair, ending in wide sideburns that reach his jawline. His mustache curves down to a thin goatee. The whole effect is reminiscent of Ché Guevara, the famous tactician of the Cuban Revolution. The man has a way of turning his face and displaying his profile, for from the side he does resemble Guevara. He certainly dresses in a manner, too, that calls attention to himself. In addition to the beret, badge of the Basque separatists, he wears an open white trenchcoat over a brown leather jacket. It is easy to signal for silence with his gun, and when he has the stage, he says melodramatically: "I am the famous Carlos."

This man calling himself Carlos was named and committed at birth to the role of a Marxist revolutionary, and so he grew up in a role and with a drama to play out. His father, a Venezuelan communist lawyer who became wealthy through real estate speculation, named each of his three sons after Lenin: Vladimir, Illich, and Nickolai. Illich Ramirez Sanchez, later to be called "Carlos," was educated according to a terrorist script. Pampered in his pleasures during childhood, he was later sent by his father to Cuba to be schooled by a KGB expert, then to Moscow's Patrice Lumumba University, and he eventually had his education refined by Arab instructors in a Palestinian camp in the Middle East.

On the surface, such instruction is, of course, deadly serious, "real" in any sense of the term. On the other hand, part of the education of the terrorist inclines him or her toward fiction; for the terrorist must be motivated by his own fictions, as well as learning to manipulate the fantasies of others. As the psychoanalyst Frederick J. Hacker has written, "Many terrorist acts are demonstratively theatrical, carefully staged and choreographed for maximal dramatic impact. The emphasis on intimidation and publicity blurs the distinction between falsehood and truth, guilt and inno- cence, show and reality; the terrorist show is the reality and the provocative scandal."

Brian Jenkins, research analyst in terrorism at the Rand Corporation and advisor to the U.S. State Department on political conspiracy and violence, phrased this more suc- cinctly: "Terrorism is theater." He argues convincingly that this is so because "terrorism is aimed at the people watching," usually on television, "not at the actual victims." The most striking example of terrorism conceived, planned, and exe- cuted so as to achieve maximum theatrical effect occurred on September 5, 1972, when eight Black September terrorists galvanized an estimated 800 million spectators by taking eleven Israeli athletes hostage at the Olympic Games in Mu- nich. While the declared demand was that the hostages be exchanged for two hundred detained Palestinians, that con- crete object was far less important than the psychological effects aimed at. One Arab terrorist explained:

> We recognize that sport is the modern religion of the Western world. We knew that the people of England and America would switch their television sets from any programme about the plight of the Palestinians if there was a sporting event on another channel. So we decided to use the Olympics, the most sacred ceremony of this religion, to make the world pay attention to us. We offered up human sacrifices to your gods of sport and television. And they answered our prayers. From Munich on- wards nobody could ignore the Palestinians or their cause.

Illich Ramirez Sanchez was nearing the end of his education in terrorism at the time of the Munich games, and he keenly grasped the lessons which it offered. When he organized and carried out the OPEC kidnapping, he clearly dressed for the part and had his lines ready. He had already taken a stage name, borrowing "Carlos" from the famous Brazilian theorist of terror, Carlos Marighella, the author of *Handbook of Urban Guerrilla Warfare*, who had been killed in 1969. Carlos was perhaps the first terrorist who understood that publicity, public exposure, and a recognizable presence all offered him benefits. The greater he grew in legend, the more powerful he became. He took command in the OPEC episode by announcing grandly to one of the ministers, "You will have heard of me already. I am the famous Carlos. You can tell that to the others."

At least so far as Austrian Chancellor Bruno Kreisky was concerned, Carlos's strategy worked perfectly—almost too well. Hearing that the ministers were held by "the famous Carlos," Kreisky was at once beset by visions of a bloodbath that would lose for Austria its reputation as a safe international conference center, and he instantly capitulated to Carlos's demands. "This Carlos is very dangerous," Kreisky said nervously. "We have heard much about him and his ruthless methods. In my opinion, we have to go along with him."

Kreisky moved so fast that Carlos felt he might be cheated out of his media show; he insisted on staying in the OPEC headquarters long enough for the television cameramen to reach the scene. He was imperious, grandiose in his sense of power. "I am the commander here," he told the negotiator. "I command Kreisky and everybody else. Nobody can tell me what to do."

Later, as he moved the hostages around the world by plane, he spent long hours spinning the yarn of his life for the benefit of Sheikh Zaki Yamani, presenting himself as a romantic playboy, beloved of women, rather like a James Bond turned terrorist. He moved around the plane in amiable, friendly fashion, chatting with his prisoners. Like Hinckley at St. Elizabeth's, he gave out autographs. "Flight Vienna to Algeria, 22–12–75, Carlos," he wrote for the minister from Nigeria. The Venezuelan oil minister, Valentin Hernandez Acosta, put it flatly: "at one moment Carlos acted like a determined killer," at the next, "he acted like a movie star." When he was not allowed to have his plane taxied to the spot reserved for Colonel Qaddafi at the Tripoli airport, he was furious, convinced that he was not being given "the proper honor." His most valued prize was yet one more—always one more—occasion for theater.

*The Day of the Jackal*, one of the best known thriller novels by Frederick Forsyth, became an international best-seller and was made into a motion picture. Whether Carlos acquired the name "the Jackal" after the main character in that book by his own instigation or because of British journalists, followed by the world press, is not clear; but the instinct to see this man through yet one more fictive screen was perfectly sound: Lenin, Carlos Marighella, Forsyth—each contributed a fragment to the identity of this man.

The emphasis upon theatricality in terrorist activity has several consequences for hostages as well. Placed in a position of dependence and usually convinced that death will soon occur, the hostage naturally begins to see the terrorist as powerful and hopes, unconsciously, to find in him evidences of kindness, idealism, and good intentions. Thus, subtly, but very quickly, the hostage begins to construct a fiction in which the terrorist and his cause have merit, while the authorities, opponents of the terrorist, begin to seem ill-intentioned, weak, even malicious. During the OPEC takeover, Carlos took Sheikh Yamani separately into an office, and "in a polite and quiet manner . . . assured me of his esteem. . . . I was listening [with gratitude] to his words, which were so incredible to me. But soon afterwards, I was to be confronted with the bitter reality of truth when he said, 'Despite our respect for you we are compelled to kill you.' " Fear, followed by gratitude, furthered by feelings of impotence accompanied by anger at the authorities who may not accede to the terrorist's demands are all present here. Then, to top it off, the terrorist made his appeal: "Carlos continued by saying that it was his desire that I should not harbor any hatred or bitterness against them for their intentions to kill me, and that, indeed, he expected a man of my intelligence to understand their noble aims and purposes."

What Carlos had done was to place Yamani in a vulnerable state in which the authorities seemed the enemies, and then he urged him to identify with the terrorists. In brief, this is the psychological formula lying behind what FBI agent Conrad Hansel and psychiatrist Frank M. Ochberg have named the "Stockholm Syndrome," after the place where its dynamics were first discerned. During a bank robbery in Stockholm in 1974, a bank employee named Kristen declared herself in love with the robber and publicly castigated the Swedish prime minister for his failure to understand her captor's point of view. Even after the ordeal Kristen professed to feel enduring affection for him.

This process, which has occurred over and over again, certainly depends upon identification—but not identification with the actual terrorist or his stated cause and real grievances; rather, the victim projects and then identifies with his or her own fictions, or with the fictions offered to him by the terrorist (Carlos's "noble aims and purposes"), with the result that identification takes place with the fictions of the captors. Into the nexus of fictions, moreover, flow all the other fictions available to the victim—from books, films, television, movies, comic strips, and so on—the cliché-ridden debris of cultural fictions.

Undoubtedly, the most notorious and widely publicized occurrence of this sort was the kidnapping and subsequent conversion to terrorism of Patricia Campbell (Patty) Hearst, daughter of Randolph Hearst. Hearst was extremely wealthy, but more important, controlled a large chain of newspapers. Kidnapping Patty, then, was not just taking any young woman prisoner, but taking an important sector of the media hostage. Patty's grandfather, William Randolph Hearst, had been a pioneer in "yellow journalism"—sensationalizing facts via fiction. Now a small group of urban guerrillas calling themselves the Symbionese Liberation Army went all the way with sensational myth-making. "The media princess," Frederick J. Hacker writes, "was a prize catch. Her possession guaranteed that the terrorist's print-in-full requirements would be carried out with utmost accuracy, thereby elevating a small, anonymous, insignificant group to the status of a strong, internationally known, and feared army." This is to say, the SLA remained the same, but the fictions attached to the group changed. This had real consequences in the final confrontation between the SLA and the police, when the police acted with a force appropriate to that for subduing a large, well-equipped, professionally expert army, instead of the handful of semi-professional activists they faced.

It had consequences, too, for Patty. Dragged out of her Berkeley apartment kicking and screaming, Patty soon appeared transformed into another person, one created by her captors, but also driven by her own vague, romantic fictions of revolution, rags and tags of images that she had picked up in Berkeley and doubtless, even from her own family's newspapers. On April 15, 1974, she was filmed in the act of robbing a bank. She soon emerged, in her new identity, with a new name, Tania, meant to identify her with Ché Guevara's Russian girl friend. The leader of the SLA, Donald DeFreeze, had been "born again" and had taken a new name, "Cinque," after a leader of a slave rebellion; but he also dressed in the manner of Ché. On tape recordings, Patty spoke a new language: referring to the putrid disease of "fucked up" bourgeois thinking and to all authorities, even her "former" family, as "pigs and fascists." She proclaimed her passionate love for Cujo, one of the SLA members.

Initially kidnapped, Patty, when arrested five hundred

and ninety-one days later, was as intent upon eluding the authorities as she would have once been in evading her kidnappers. A friend who talked to her said that she seemed "very different, dazed and disoriented." She was still Tania, still living in her acquired fictions. In her case, what started as a real event soon became riddled with fictions and ended as a full-blown media event, culminating in hundreds of articles, nearly a score of books, and several movies devoted to enshrining the episode as the newest subgenre of romance.

Patricia Campbell Hearst's book, *Every Secret Thing*, her own account (written with Alvin Moscow) of her life in the SLA, gives a vivid, if too often self-justifying account of the way that a set of convincing fictions can drive reality, especially the reality of one's own identity, out of consciousness. Several episodes in the book merit examination.

Shortly after Patty was allowed to leave the closet in which she had been isolated, "Field Marshall" Cinque lined up the people in the apartment. When he came to Hearst he barked: "Who are you?" She was bewildered.

> I did not have the slightest idea of what he was talking about or what he wanted.
>
> "I said, 'Who are you?' Who are you," he hissed.
>
> "I don't know what you mean."
>
> "You're a guerilla fighter! You're a soldier in the Symbionese Liberation Army. Now you say it. I'll ask you again: 'Who are you?' "
>
> "I am a guerilla fighter, a soldier in the Symbionese Liberation Army," I declared as fiercely as I could.
>
> "Good," said he. "Now you remember that!"

Her reeducation had begun. She was being told that her identity existed in her association with a group. But the group itself had no natural existence. It was a purely artificial construct, with innumerable invented rituals, rules, mythologies, guiding principles, symbols, hierarchies, history, and so on, a great melange of fiction and clichés derived and imitated from a wide variety of sources. Immediately following this exchange, Patty is taught "the SLA salute, which was a clenched fist thumped over and away from the heart." Here she began to acquire the fictions that eventually were to displace her own identity.

Each member of the SLA was given a special name, another ritual meant to indicate that the old personal identity had been obliterated. Hearst tells how this occurred in her case.

> Cin also christened me with my revolutionary name in the SLA. It came casually and caught me by surprise. He simply announced: "We got to come up with a new name for you." He thought for not more than a moment or so and then added: "We're going to call you Tania. She was a guerilla, a wonderful guerilla fighter with Ché Guevara in Bolivia." He handed me a book and said, "Here, you read this and you'll see she was right on." The book was *Tania: The Unforgettable Guerilla*, and I immediately started to flip through the pages. I vastly preferred to read a book by myself than to be forced into any of their more strenuous activities.

This renaming has a vaguely mythological quality to it, as if by taking the name of a deceased heroine, one could acquire some of her strength or dedication. On a more practical level, Patty is asked directly to read, identify with, and imitate a fiction.

By the time she was apprehended by the FBI, she had absorbed a wholly new identity, based on imitation of radical fictions. Her thoughts as she was brought to the FBI headquarters where the press was waiting, were purely: how should a "revolutionary" act? What gestures should a "revolutionary" make? What radical models are appropriate?

> As the flashbulbs went off in my face, I remembered the press pictures of Susan Saxe, a revolutionary who had recently been arrested, and like her, I smiled broadly and raised a clenched fist in salute. This is how I'm supposed to act now, I thought. Those pictures would show me being taken off to a fascist concen-

tration camp, like a true revolutionary. I had a role to play and I knew my part well.

At this time, she says, she felt "as though I were outside everything, floating through a surrealistic Jean Cocteau film." The whole portrayal of her identity looks as if it were being directed by someone else, and her actions are based upon a script composed for her: she is merely an actress.

Before her trial, she had a psychiatric evaluation and was described as having suffered a "traumatic neurosis with dissociative features" caused by powerful "coercive manipulation by her captors." The well-known psychoanalyst, Dr. Robert J. Lifton, pronounced her "a classic case" of mental coercion, resembling that of prisoners of war. As the trial showed, Hearst was not the only one caught up in fictions, however. "It was the media image of me on trial," she remarked. Perhaps she *was*, at last, only a media image. Certainly the media helped to keep her a fiction.

During the last decade the FBI has increasingly used undercover agents against drug dealers, terrorist groups, racketeers, and others. These agents begin by constructing identities, learning roles, playing at perspectives upon reality different from their own. Physical danger is present, of course; but by the early 1980s a greater danger was showing up with sufficient regularity that FBI officials were moved to commission a study of the problem: many agents, once having assumed a false identity, found it difficult, if not impossible, to shed the fictions after the undercover assignment was completed. The false role became the true self. In 1983, FBI Director William H. Webster sent a memo to field supervisors warning them to be on the lookout for personality changes in undercover agents. The very same elements of personality that make an agent able to play a part are the ones that make it difficult for him or her to shed the role.

A few examples are sufficient to show the problem in a clear light. Between 1982 and 1983, FBI agent Dan A. Mitrone began an undercover investigation of narcotics smuggling at the Fort Lauderdale, Florida, airport. Set up as an expert on debugging under the name of Dan Micelli, Mitrone made numerous contacts with airline pilots who were concerned about eavesdropping on their smuggling activities. Eventually, however, Mitrone conspired with an informer to close a big cocaine deal, from which he himself netted $850,000. So, finally, Mitrone himself, the undercover agent, was the only criminal caught in the covert operation. He had gotten trapped in his fictions and then acted them out. Convicted of drug dealing and bribery, Mitrone, his wife says, "doesn't know why he acted the way he did. The only thing he said was . . . 'It wasn't me . . . I had to try so hard to be this guy [Micelli] that it wasn't me.' "

An even more dramatic instance of the way a fictive identity can get fixed even in a personality that chooses it, involved another FBI agent, Pat Livingston. As "Pat Salamone," he posed as a hustler interested in dealing in pornography in the Miami area. The requirements of the role were heavy. Six months passed before the suspicious Mafia men who were the operation's targets were convinced of "Salamone's" and his partner's "legitimacy." Anthony M. DeStefano, a journalist who followed the case, writes:

> For nearly three years, the pair acted their roles, eating in expensive restaurants, jetting coast to coast for sex-film conventions, palling around with mobsters and picking up women. . . . Mr. Livingston came to know his targets not only as suspects but also as ordinary men with conventional hopes and concerns for their families and their business ventures.
>
> In 1981, the "Miporn" (or Miami pornography) investigation ended with the indictment of 45 persons for conspiring to ship pornographic books and films around the country. But even during the euphoria of success, Mr. Livingston couldn't relin-

quish "Pat Salamone." He continued to visit his old bars, book-makers and various hangers-on he had come to know, even though most by then knew he was an FBI agent, says Miami lawyer William Brown, a friend of Mr. Livingston. "He maintained a bank account of Pat Salamone, a driver's license, and was making out he was very happy to be known as Pat Salamone," Mr. Brown says.

After this case was completed, Livingston returned to his home office in Lexington, Kentucky, where he took another undercover assignment, using the name and identity of — "Pat Salamone." Not long after, he was arrested for shoplifting, and identified himself as Pat Salamone. Eventually, he was fired by the FBI.

The greatest terrorist of modern times was certainly Joseph Stalin. In the first volume of his biography of Stalin, *Stalin as Revolutionary*, Robert C. Tucker gives a stunning example of how a neurotic character structure developed in Stalin, how it influenced his career as a revolutionary, and how it profoundly affected the whole of Russian society following Stalin's consolidation of his power after the death of Lenin. Moreover, in a recent essay, "A Stalin Biographer's Memoir," Tucker has written a personal account of how he came to understand Stalin's neuroses as—in my phrase—that of fictive personality.

Tucker was a member of the diplomatic corps from 1945 to 1953. At the time that the final statement of Karen Horney's psychoanalytic views was published in her 1950 book *Neurosis and Human Growth,* Tucker was serving in the American embassy in Moscow. Horney's understanding of neurosis involved her in developmental considerations. She argued that a person who experiences significant emotional distress in early life is likely to develop a "basic anxiety" that remains fearful even after the events which caused the early distress have ceased. As a defense against "basic anxiety," the person may form an "idealized image" of himself or herself—that is to say, the child creates a fiction, a superman image, of his perfection. If the inner pressure of anxiety continues over a long duration, this self-idealizing defense will gradually evolve into an "idealized self," an image and imaginary or fictive identity—*not* the real identity, but a fiction of one. What Horney calls the "search for glory" consists of the attempt to force the world to acknowledge the "idealized 'f'" as the real self.

orney, then, is describing the creation of a rigid self as ction against basic fear. Such a self, if it is to be tective, can have no flaws, no human limitations. must be invulnerable. Others must also accept e "idealized self," or the protection is threatened. hose adulation is so desperately needed, must *They* are fallible, merely human, potential herwise insignificant. The "idealized self" eption. The "idealized self" is right; all nd their errors are threatening to the be created should the idealized self ress others and have its own way. hat are repressed and disavowed y are projected onto others— to be hated; they are to be lorney writes, the idealized umph" over any persons supremacy of the ideal-

of personality that ked himself, "the fter day in the re *an idealized* many other wer unprec must ref

Stalin's own monstrously inflated vision of himself as the greatest genius of Russian and world history. The cult must be an institutionalization of his neurotic character structure." Things fell into place. Stalin's ruthless suppression of colleagues, his infusion of himself into all institutions of Soviet society, his inability to tolerate dissent, all pointed to a drive toward mastery through the elimination of all values but his own. He had, Tucker concluded, used his enormous power to gain almost total control, mobilizing the resources of a totalitarian state to repress his "enemies," to scorn mere human claims, and to install himself as the central ideal and all-wise hero of an entire society.

To defend against a basic dread, young Stalin learned to make a fiction about himself. Then, during the revolution he found a body of materials by which he could shape himsel the writings of Marx, Lenin, and others, along with t romance of the revolution, all gave him purpose and an im of himself as powerful, so special a person that he c help to overthrow a czar and then replace Lenin, the f of the revolution. Thus the boy Josif Dzhugashvili, sub to a dismal early life and repeatedly beaten by his d father, found a new family in communism and a new name, "Stalin," man of steel. He would rescue Rus victimization by the czar, as if the czar were a bad father who beat his children. But beneath the def vided by the fictions of "The Revolutionary" s the old anxiety, self-doubts, anger at authority of rivals that led to the young Stalin's anger place.

This, indeed, was Nikita Khrushchev's vie in his secret report to the Twentieth Party Cd in *The New York Times* as "On the Cult of its Consequences." In this document Khr talin as grandiose, insecure, subject to rag ious reassurance, arrogant but uncerta gry for glory yet scorning those from whom he received it. In Khrushchev's view, Stalin's drive to self-glorification and his frequent purges were but two sides of the same character structure. In the drama of The Revolution, a young man who had been terrorized as a boy found a heroic position for himself and a way of punishing, by proxy, those who had tyrannized him. But his fiction still carried the old fright, and was transformed into the terrorization of others.

The best exploration of the processes involved in the diffusion of an old identity by infusion of the fictions of a new identity in terrorism is in John le Carré's novel *The Little Drummer Girl*. As le Carré's foreword makes clear, the novel was based on extensive firsthand research in Israel, Sidon, Beirut, and the Palestinian training camps at Rashidiyeh and Nabatiyeh. The novel concerns a young English actress, Charmian (probably after Jack London's famous wife, but also alluding to "chameleon"), or "Charlie." She is a good actress precisely because she has a weak sense of self. The stories that she tells about herself are pure inventions of her sense of theatrical appropriateness. She allies her own history with the major fictions of her time—she has played at being "a militant pacifist, a sufist, a nuclear marcher, an anti-vivisectionist, and . . . a champion of campaigns to eliminate tobacco from the underground." An acquaintance of hers says: "Actors don't have *opinions*, my dear chap, still less do actresses. They have moods. Fads. Poses. Twenty-four hour passions. . . . Actors are absolute suckers for dramatic solutions. For all I know, by the time you get her out there, she'll be Born Again!" He went further and showed how actors "were pursued by 'an absolute *horror* of unreality.' How on stage they acted out all the agonies of man, and off stage were hollow vessels waiting to be filled."

An Israeli special forces anti-terrorist team recruits Charlie with the special goal of filling her emptiness with a new role. Their aim is to locate and kill a wily Palestinian terrorist. For Charlie they construct an elaborate drama in which she "becomes" the girl friend of the terrorist's brother; the special forces team compose a history of their love affair, complete with love letters between them. She is "filled up" with a complete set of political advocacies, acquaintances, a lover, and a mission. As Kurtz, the head of the Israeli team, tells her, she is being given a role in "the theater of the real." She takes in her new fictive identifications so readily that they do indeed become part of her identity—they *are* her identity, she becomes her fictions, for they are as real as anything else in her life has been.

Near the end of the novel, having passed all the tests by which the Palestinians confirm for themselves that her fictive identity is real, she makes contact with the terrorist, Khalil. "He was everything she had imagined when she was trying to turn him into somebody she was looking forward to meeting." Together they assemble a bomb, which she is scheduled to use in an assassination.

> "You are nervous?" Khalil asks.
> "Yes."
> "It's natural. I too am nervous. Are you nervous in the theater?"
> "Yes."
> "It is the same. Terror is theater. We inspire. We frighten, we awaken indignation, anger, love. We enlighten. The theater also. The guerilla is the great actor of the world."

Toward the book's end, after the bombing, "It was the worst play she had ever been in," she thinks.

After Khalil is killed, Charlie is given brief psychiatric care at a sanitarium, along with new fictions to explain her absence from London and the large sum of money she has acquired. Then she is returned to the theater. But the tragic plays make her cry in panic, and the comedies seem wholly irrelevant. She is stuck, and neither reality nor other fictions will do for her.

Charlie is an actress, a good one, but not a great one. She is good because she can so easily adopt whatever role is offered to her, but not great because her own identity is insufficient. That prevents her from powerfully infusing an authentic personality of her own into her roles. Subsequently, in Chapter Six I will explore the relation between modern acting theory, actors, and fictive personality. Those people whom I have investigated in this chapter are not "real" actors, but actors in the theater of the real. They play out fictions in a truly dangerous way—for themselves and for others. Their stage is the daily newspaper, where the strange, terrifying, brutal fictions of our time have their terrible scripts and violent denouements.

# 4

# Don Quixote and His Heirs

While Terry, the patient described earlier, obliged me to notice fictions and their operations in personality, another patient, Melissa, continued my education. Melissa was an unmarried woman in her early twenties when I first saw her. Fairly early in treatment she began to explore the idea that understanding the world required three keys. Her theory was that the world had three shapes, corresponding to her three favorite books—*Little Women*, *Gone with the Wind*, and *The Wizard of Oz*. One had only to select the appropriate book and passage to interpret whatever aspect of the world a problem brought to hand, and the way of dealing with it would become evident. Never mind if the way of dealing didn't work: the "key" remained right, though the world might be wrong.

It was no accident that lost girls were at the heart of all

these books—in Jo, Scarlett, and Dorothy—alone and frightened, abandoned by men and yearning for new men, lovers
or fathers, to save them—powerful wizards or forceful bucca-
neers. "I was Daddy's girl and could do no wrong," Melissa
said, both literally and also symbolically, many times.

We soon were involved in a whirl of fictions. *Mary, Queen
of Scots*, *My Fair Lady*, and a child's book titled *Lulu's Window*
were modifications of the basic three. In all of them, the
real identity was false and the fantasized identity was really
true. "I tend to live in a fantasy world," Melissa said openly.
"I play games. I do it almost all the time when I'm alone—
for instance in my car, at night, or in the bathroom. And
of course everything turns out right. I have a sick uncle
who leaves me $50 million. I never grow old." Even in her
dreams she was in the books she was reading.

Melissa's convictions had a creative aspect. She wrote
poems and analyzed them in her sessions—*those* seemed more
truly herself than the unfamiliar self that managed a household or went to school. But mostly she used fictions to keep
reality false. When she was depressed, she whispered to
herself, "Scarlett O'Hara says, 'Tomorrow's another day!' "
She knew that she wasn't Scarlett O'Hara most times, but
she found the character irresistible and she slipped into it
whenever possible: "Her similarity to me is enormous: she
was aggressive, shocking, ungenteel. But look what was demanded of her. . . . When she needed her father most he
had an accident and broke his neck."

When Melissa felt alone, she gathered real or imaginary
friends around her—like Dorothy, in threes. (I was sometimes
cast in the role of the scarecrow, with no brains, but a friend
nonetheless.) She even saw me as playing a role, as if our
real meanings were in the characters we played. "The image
that came to me was you as the Wizard of Oz and also the
Scarecrow, who helped Dorothy," she said once. Everything
in her life could be tinged with fiction.

Henry Adams, whose autobiography makes plain that his core identity and object attachments were thoroughly fictive, wrote in 1915:

> But we, who cannot fly the world must seek
> To live two separate lives; one in the world
> Which we must ever seem to treat as real;
> The other in ourselves, behind a veil.

Melissa had treated the world *as if* it were real; now, in psychoanalysis, she began to come from behind the veil and live in the world's reality.

A reiterated complaint of Melissa's was that through the process of psychoanalytic interpretation I had robbed her of the ability to live her other fantasy lives. Her storybook guides, *Little Women*, *The Wizard of Oz*, and *Gone with the Wind*, no longer seemed to explain everything. She still yearned for fictions, but she began to find that she could do without them. During final exams in school, she expressed her ambivalence about fictions, along with a growing understanding of their influence upon her. She said, "When I'm studying for exams I need some kind of release—for instance, I'm reading Agatha Christie's mysteries. I know what it is about the mysteries: it's the whole way of life. The characters in her stories are wealthy and can do as they please. I conjure up a vision of people out on lawns sipping lemonade on a storybook day. I would absolutely love to live in that fashion, with enough money so that I wouldn't have to do anything I didn't want to do, and working could be a hobby. That's what I'd *like*. I'd like not to be under all these compulsions. Then I go back to studying, and it's o.k."

Not long after making this crucial distinction between fantasies that supplant reality and fantasies of power that helpfully release anxiety, Melissa reported a dream that began with all sorts of scary adventures, during which she hid in a suitcase. "After a while I climbed out of the suitcase, but

I came out of the tail of a plane that had crashed: the tail was still sticking out of the water. I swam away. I wasn't sure which direction to take, but I decided to go east and thought, 'I'll just lie on my back and relax.' People came and they started to show *The Wizard of Oz*. I see the witch flying away. I realize it was all a fake, that I had been in a movie."

In her associations she said: "After all her adventures Dorothy wakes up and finds it was all a dream, and she says, 'There's no place like home.' That's just me. Analysis has been a good adventure, and fantasies that once seemed real I know now are only fantasies. I feel like I've been born again and can get a real home now." This was the first step in the good conclusion to analysis that Melissa eventually made. She learned that she could move under her own power, and she no longer needed to see the world in terms of Dorothy's story. The witches flew away. Melissa could begin to make her own story, as well as to see her past life as like a movie.

Melissa's use of an identification with Dorothy always gave us signals about where she was in her analytic story. *The Wizard of Oz* is one of those tales that in our time has acquired an especially powerful relation to inner life. One of the few items found in Mark Chapman's hotel room after the Lennon shooting was a still photograph from *The Wizard of Oz*, showing Judy Garland wiping a tear from the cheek of the cowardly lion. Baum's story has a multiplicity of appeals. Reflecting on the modeling power and organizing effects of fictions, Nancy C. A. Roeske has written interestingly on *The Wizard of Oz* as a work whose understanding will be influenced by gender:

> The heroine, Dorothy, learns that, although powerful environmental forces can at times control her, she has the power within her to decide and get what she wants. Before she learns this lesson, she learns that males, in the forms of a scarecrow, a

tin woodman, and a lion, need to attain visible signs of intelligence, a heart, and courage from a "bald-headed, wrinkled old
man" in order to feel adequate. They cannot rely on an inner
conviction of these attributes. She learns that a population can
be controlled by the tricks of a magician, a man who admits
he is a "humbug." She learns that the scarecrow, the tin woodman, and the lion feel indebted to her for helping them find
their prized attributes. She learns that the Wizard cannot rescue
her; in fact, she sews the balloon that rescues him from Oz.
Finally, it is Glinda, the good witch, who tells Dorothy about
her power of standing on her own two feet and clicking her
heels to get what she wants. Dorothy chooses to go home to a
dour Uncle Henry and an unsmiling Aunt Em. The story of
Dorothy continues to be one of the most widely read books in
the United States. Does that fact have any meaning for the
evolving American female?

Roeske's description is close to many of Melissa's feelings
at the end of her analysis. In contrast to Charlie of *The
Little Drummer Girl*, who ends the book saying, over and
over, "I am dead," Melissa started to make new identifications—with me, and with her family background, a new
profession, and friends.

The way that Melissa turned naturally to literature in
order to give herself temporary inner structure—however
rigid and useless that might eventually prove to be—reminded
me that writers had first discovered the process that captured
my interest, and I began increasingly to explore how they
dealt with it. Perhaps the first great examples of this personality process in literature are Paolo and Francesca, whom Dante
addresses in Canto V of the *Inferno*, asking how these two
came to sin through love. Francesca answers that they followed out of the prescriptions of a book.

> One day together read we for good cheer
> Of Love, how he laid hold on Launcelot:

Alone we were and without any fear.
Many and many a time that reading brought
Our eyes to meet, and blanched our faces o'er.
But only one point we resisted not,
When reading of the smile long-waited for
Being kissed by such a lover chivalrous,
He, never now from me divided more,
Kissed me upon the mouth all tremulous.
Gallehaut was the book and writer too:
That day there was no reading more for us.

Dante is suggesting, of course, something about the psychological witchery of reading—especially, in his own time, the popular reading of romance. Paolo and Francesca were, it must be presumed, educated in morals and able to distinguish between the legitimate and sinful uses of sexuality. But their moral selves were displaced by the intrusions of their romantic identification with a book, and the "fictive" behavior that followed committed them to a course of unending, undying passionate love which continued even in hell. Their romantic fiction permanently drove out their moral identities.

The story of Paolo and Francesca is a quick sketch in Dante, albeit a very famous one. A full portrait is, however, given in one of the world's enduring literary characters, Don Quixote. In this outstanding character Cervantes gives us a remarkable, full exhibition of the fictive personality, and he helps thereby to enlarge our sense of the way fictions become imbedded. In its most general sense, the theme of the book is the confusion between illusion or fantasy and reality. Waldo Frank expresses it well when he says Don Quixote is "a man possessed, not a madman." What has "possessed" him is clear: his personality has been seized, captured, filled up by the literature of chivalry. As one of Cervantes's prefatory poems to the novel has it, the Don is

> a Manchegan gentleman whose reading
> Had turned his head with tales of bleeding
> Knights-errant, damsels, love's surprises,
> And all the Chivalry's disguises.

He becomes so addicted to such reading that in order to buy books he sells off large parcels of his estate—"so great," Cervantes writes, "was his curiosity and infatuation" with chivalric tales. "In short, our gentleman became so immersed in his reading that he spent whole nights from sundown to sunup and his days from dawn to dusk in poring over books, until finally, from so little sleeping and so much reading. . . . [he] had filled his imagination with everything he had read . . . all sorts of impossible things, and as a result had come to believe that all these fictitious happenings were true; they were more real to him than anything else in the world."

Don Quixote's mind becomes so filled with his fictions that these dislodge his previous grip on reality. His "habit of reading books of chivalry with such pleasure and devotion. . . . led him almost wholly to forget the life of a hunter and the administration of his estate." At last, "he came to conceive the strangest idea that ever occurred to any madman in this world"—he would go in quest of adventures, by way of "putting into practice all that he had read in his books."

To accompany his new being, he had to get a horse and give it a proper name. Then he had to give himself a new name, as the romance-knight Amadis of Gaul had done. "Having found a name for his horse that pleased his fancy, he then desired to do as much for himself, and this required another week, and by the end of that period he had made up his mind that he was henceforth to be known as Don Quixote. . . . But remembering that the valiant knight Amadis was not content to call himself that and nothing more, but added the name of his kingdom and fatherland that he might make it famous also, and thus came to take the name Amadis of Gaul, so our good knight chose to add his place of origin and become 'Don Quixote de la Mancha'; for by this means, as he saw it, he was making very plain his lineage and was conferring honor upon his country by taking its name as his own." Finally he had to find a lady to whom he could consecrate his efforts.

All this activity is based on the traditions of chivalric literature, whose "authority and prestige" Cervantes said he had written the book to overthrow. The Don swallows the romantic tradition whole. He seems bewitched. The curate, barber, and his housekeeper gain entrance to Don Quixote's study and sprinkle holy water about the room, then they burn his vast collection of romances, as if they could thereby exorcise the demon possessing Don Quixote's person. But the "demon" is his personality and the books live on, as fictions, in him.

Literary critics, philosophers, psychoanalysts, and all of us, in an ordinary, normal way, recognize that the power of fictions resides in their ability to promote identifications. Fictions are central to growth and creativity. But in the personality I am looking at, the identification has a completely different quality, seeming almost to amount to possession. The identification does not stop at resemblance—it becomes total, incorporating the violent and depressive aspects of the fictional character without self-examination, in a completely unscrutinized, indiscriminate manner. Fictions do not simulate life, they are a *source* of life.

Don Quixote reassumes his mundane appearance just in time to die, after eight hundred pages. It is a comedic book. But some of the serious implications—already evident in the Don's violence, distortions, and omnipotence—are also clear as they bubble just beneath the comedic surface.

In 1937 Helene Deutsch published an interesting article, "Don Quixote and Don Quixotisms," in which she understands his behavior as a regression to the onset of sexuality at puberty. "Disillusioned, mortified, humiliated, Alonzo withdraws from life in a riot of inferiority feelings, and gradually, in the course of days and nights undoubtedly fraught with anxiety and depression, his real personality vanishes. In fantasy, that activity which causes reality to disappear, there is born in place of the mortal Alonzo the immortal Don Quixote. All the threads which once linked Alonzo with the material world are severed." In regressing to adolescence, she argues, then, Don Quixote renews his boyhood fascination with romantic literature and thereby also finds a way, in adulthood, to compensate for his lack of sexual experience and gratification. Ordinarily, at puberty, the boy abandons the world of magic in favor of reality; Don Quixote, on the contrary, "betakes himself into the depths of a still longer forgotten past, into the practice of a magic whereby the young child, like the savage, is himself able to cast a spell over the things of the material world, and himself believes in this enchantment."

What Deutsch seems to miss and certainly minimizes is the doubleness of the appeal of Don Quixote to the reader. As the "big child" whom in essence she is describing, he is a comic figure; as a person who enhances fictions to noble sentiments and gives them a high dignity, he endows himself with wisdom and nobility, and becomes, as Freud wrote in 1905, "the symbolic representative of an idealism which believes in the realization of its aims and takes duties seriously and takes promises literally. . . ." Don Quixote is a big child—and also a noble hero with the wisdom of the ancients.

While Cervantes fuses the noble with the comic in Don Quixote, Johann Wolfgang von Goethe, in *The Sorrows of Young Werther*, brings together the idealistic and the tragic. *The Sorrows of Young Werther* presents a complicated situation. Summarized in the briefest possible way, it is the story of a reflective, melancholy young man, Werther, who falls in love with an unattainable woman, Charlotte, and, in the end—unable to win her love—turns his romantic passion into an active passion for death and commits suicide. At the core of Werther's being is a conviction of helpless emptiness. "I enjoy no single moment of happiness," he writes to Charlotte: "all is vain—nothing touches me. I stand, as it were, before a circus show. I see the little puppets move, and I ask whether it is not an optical illusion. I am amused with these puppets, or rather, I am myself one of them." On his own, he says, "I wish for nothing—I have no desires." Charlotte, wisely, but in vain, advises him to "seek and find an object worthy of your love."

The problem is, Werther already has found an object of imitation to fill up his empty personality—but that object is a fiction. He does not love Charlotte; he is, when he exists, not Werther. He sees himself as a character in a novel; specifically, he comes into existence as Saint-Preux, the romantic lover in Rousseau's novel *The New Heloise*, published thirteen years before Goethe's novel. Like Saint-Preux, Werther gives up his conventional clothes—his social role, in essence—and dons Saint-Preux's costume, a famous blue coat and yellow vest. He *can* wear a disguise without meeting frustration. Werther's mistake consists in trying to cast the "real" Charlotte in the role of Rousseau's fictional character Julie.

So Werther attempts to force a fiction upon reality, and the force of that need leads to frustration, anger, depression, and eventually suicide. Complicating the picture still further is the fact that *The New Heloise* itself originally arose from, and obviously incorporated into itself, Rousseau's own feeling that reality had become a fantasy. In one of his letters Rousseau describes this feeling very clearly: "I had not yet found a friend entirely to myself, a true friend. . . . Devoured by this need to love without having been able to satisfy it, I saw myself reaching the gates of old age, and dying without having lived." As a defense against this feeling of fictiveness,

he wrote his novel: "The impossibility of reaching real creatures threw me into the land of fantasies. . . . which my
creative imagination soon populated with creatures after my
own heart. . . . [I made] an enchanted world."

Goethe himself wore Saint-Preux's famous costume when
he lived at Wetzlar, and he too wrote a book to sublimate
elements of his own self. But Werther, the character, was
given no such creative outlet, and his commitment to fictions
drives him straight to suicide. What is more, the situation
that followed the publication of the book offers the first
modern instance of a phenomenon that would occur over
and over in modern culture. George Brandes (1936) tells
how "young men sympathized, first in Germany, and later
in many other countries, with Werther: they dressed and
yearned and felt as he did. Young women wanted to be
loved just as Lotte had been loved." Many of them committed
suicide in complete identification with him. Werther gave
scores of people an identity and a role to play—but the
role ended in suicide. Goethe was aware of this and told
his friend Eckermann: "Werther belongs to the life-process
of every individual who . . . seeks to find himself and adapt
to the restrictive forms of a world grown old. Thwarted
happiness, hampered activity, ungratified desires—these are
not the infirmities of a particular [historical] period, but those
of every single human being, and it must be sad if each
should not once have had a phase in his life when Werther
affected him as if it were written only for him." Napoleon,
it might be noted, taken by Werther's narcissistic grandiosity,
brought the book on his Egyptian campaign and read it
seven times.

Many other books come to mind in which the main theme
is the way in which an empty, narcissistic person, or sometimes a child in whom identity formation has scarcely begun,
"imports" into the self a character from fiction or history.
In *Wuthering Heights*, Cathy says, "I am Heathcliff." Emma

Bovary, in Flaubert's novel, identifies with a whole series of romantic heroines. In *Crime and Punishment*, Raskolnikov wants to be, then acts as if he is, a Napoleon-like superman. In *Adventures of Huckleberry Finn*, Huck imitates Tom Sawyer, and Tom bases his actions upon the heroes of romantic adventure novels. Walker Percy's *The Moviegoer* exhibits the effects of film fictions upon personality. Klaus Mann's *Mefisto* (based on his brother-in-law) is about an actor, Hofgen, who, because he wants nothing more than to have roles to play, collaborates with the Nazis. The novel ends with Hofgen weeping in his mother's arms, bewildered by the demands of reality, crying: "What do men want of me? I am only an actor." Mario Puig's *Rita Hayworth* and *The Kiss of the Spider Woman* are exacting portrayals of personalities that achieve definition wholly through fictions.

These are just some of the heirs of *Don Quixote*. On its own, *Don Quixote* has spawned scores of sequels and imitators. Graham Greene, in *Monsignor Quixote*, writes about a simple priest in Spain, Father Quixote, who, it is rumored, is a descendant of Don Quixote.

> "How can he be descended from a fictional character?" the Bishop demands, with evident scorn for the country priest.
> "A fictional character?"
> "A character [the Bishop explains] in a novel by an overrated writer called Cervantes—a novel moreover with many disgusting passages which in the days of the generalissimo would not even have passed the censor."
> "But, Your Excellency, you can see the house of Dulcinea in El Toboso. There [it] is marked on a plaque. . . ."

The Bishop says impatiently that the house is not really one in which a woman named Dulcinea lived—it is an "invented" house, a commercial illusion, a "trap for tourists" who believe that fictions are true.

But in the character of Father Quixote, Greene shows

that "fictions" can truly make the personality. Father Quixote's equivalents to his "ancestor's" books of chivalry are
his books of the spiritual life—St. John of the Cross, St.
Teresa, St. Francis de Sales, and the Gospels. Greene is
suggesting that to most people such spiritual works now
seem as improbable and fantastical as books of romance.
By a curious chance Father Quixote becomes a monsignor
by the Pope's order; and free from his duties and the com-
mands of his bishop, he goes on adventures in the company
of an earthy believer in Marx and Lenin, a materialist like
Don Quixote's Sancho Panza. Like his ancestor, he tries to
live up to ideals that seem to have fallen completely out of
fashion. To everyone else he is living a fictive life; only he
knows that he is truly living in the reality of ideals. So
Greene stands the Quixote tradition on its head. Monsignor
Quixote perceives reality; nearly everyone else in twentieth-
century culture is a shallow fiction.

The vivid portrayals of fictive personalities in novels should
not blind us to the fact that the theme often appears on
the stage. Luigi Pirandello's play *Six Characters in Search of
an Author* expresses in its very title concern about finding
roles to play, and this work is justly famous. But Pirandello's
play of the following year, *Henry IV*, is an even more profound
exploration of lives that are invented. Both show, as Pirandello suggested, "the theater as the theater," illusion taking
the place of reality, fictions imitating fictions.

The play opens upon a group of characters who are dressed
in the style of the court at Goslar of Henry IV of Germany,
in the middle of the eleventh century. But another time
dimension and another place are immediately apparent: we
are also in the twentieth century, in Italy. The men on
stage are actors hired to play parts compatible with the delusions and attendant demands of a wealthy but mad Italian.
Years before, during a masquerade and pageant in which

he was playing Henry IV, he fell from his horse onto his head, and became stuck in his illusion. He has turned his whole household, then, into fictions—with costumes, suitable parts to play, new roles, period decorations, and so on.

As audience, we see on the stage a complicated situation: men and women who are actors and actresses playing parts in the present; but these performers are also playing the parts given to them by a madman's delusion. All four layers of identity are called forth by the play's theme. The Doctor, to take this a step further, claims that Henry cannot be perfectly deluded: one split-off part of his mind must know who he really is: "We must take into account the peculiar psychology of madmen [who] . . . . can in fact recognize the disguise and yet believe in it; just as children do, for whom disguise is both play and reality." Then, to complicate matters still further, Henry himself steps forth and claims that he is really not mad at all. He has been only "playing the madman," "having a joke on those that think I'm mad!" He ends the play, however, with the declaration that he prefers madness to sanity and fictions to reality. "Now, Doctor," he exclaims, "the case must be absolutely new in the history of madness; I preferred to remain mad—since I found everything ready and at my disposal for this new exquisite fantasy. I would live it—this madness of mine—with the most lucid consciousness." He is cured of madness, he says, "because I can act the madman to perfection."

In the 1980s, the comic aspects of Pirandello's dramatic visions are best continued in the work of Woody Allen, in his three-fold activities as actor, writer, and director. One of Allen's most interesting short stories is a highly condensed symbolic and comic comment on the process I have been describing.

"The Kugelmass Episode" is a fantasy about what can happen when one lives out a fiction. Sidney Kugelmass, a professor of humanities at City College, tells his analyst that he needs an affair in order to bring excitement to his life. Disappointingly, his analyst offers him only reality, and Kugelmass turns to an inventor in the Bushwick section of Brooklyn to fulfill his desires. The man, it seems, has created a wonderful new machine. He explains to Kugelmass that he must sit in a cabinet, and then—"if I throw any novel into this cabinet with you, shut the doors and tap it three times, you will find yourself projected into that book. . . . You can meet any of the women created by the world's best authors. . . . So, who do you want to meet? Sister Carrie? Hester Prynne? Ophelia? Maybe somebody by Saul Bellow? Hey, what about Temple Drake?"

Eventually, Kugelmass decides upon Emma Bovary. He is transported to her house—while Charles is away—and they become lovers. He notices that she speaks in the same fine English translation as the paperback. And he is delighted. ("My God," he thinks. "I'm doing it with Madame Bovary. . . . Me, who failed Freshman English.") But after he gets the bright idea of bringing Emma back with him into the modern world, things start to fall apart. She runs up large bills. She is a drag on his hands and a drain on his resources. He tries to get her back to nineteenth-century France and only after a great amount of trouble finally succeeds. The moral here is that it is all right to live occasionally with fictions, but to bring them into reality—and to have them stay with you at the Plaza!—is quite another thing.

Two of Allen's recent movies provide further explorations of fictive processes. The first is *Zelig* and the second *The Purple Rose of Cairo;* one is about a man, the other a woman, and they thus make a connected pair of gender-defined films.

*Zelig* is structured like a research project in psychohistory. The film's narrator asks: who was this now forgotten but once prominent man Leonard Zelig, "who created such diverse impressions?" Various photographic records, documents, newspaper headlines, newsreels, and motion-picture excerpts are assembled; research into diaries and memoirs is undertaken, and interviews are conducted both of those "witnesses" who knew Zelig and also of those whose skill as social critics might enable them to give accurate insights into the strange phenomenon represented by Zelig. He is a man who seems to have no personality of his own, not even a constant physical appearance. He simply takes on the ideas, values, skills, appearance, manner, and even physiognomy of the people he is with. F. Scott Fitzgerald assumes he is a writer. In the company of Babe Ruth, he becomes a slugger. At a speakeasy party he looks black when he joins the band to play the trumpet, but out in the audience with members of the mafia, it seems that he is a hoodlum. Later he appears to be Chinese in Chinatown, and becomes fat when around fat men. On St. Patrick's Day he becomes Irish. His psychiatrist at first mistakes him for a colleague, rather than a patient, for in her presence he impersonates a physician to perfection.

Little by little, the etiology of his illness emerges. His psychoanalyst, Dr. Eudora Fletcher, asks: "Tell me why you assume the characteristics of those you are with." Under hypnosis Zelig says that first, it gives him a feeling of safety; and second, he wants to be liked, and he is accepted by those he resembles. Certainly, the confusing messages in his early relation to his parents and family contributed to his need for defenses and his narcissistic wounds. His father was a Yiddish actor who took the side of anti-Semites! His sociopathic siblings beat him. The message his father gave him was: "Life is a meaningless nightmare," and his advice was: "Save string." At twelve years old, Zelig asked a rabbi the meaning of life—but the answer was given in Hebrew.

According to the fiction of the movie, Zelig, "the human who transforms himself," was a public sensation. A film based on his life was made, and he had tremendous popular impact. He was endlessly discussed—but, not surprisingly—each commentator saw in Zelig a reflection of his or her own preoccupations. French intellectuals saw him as a symbol of everything. Susan Sontag considered him from a socio-aesthetic point of view. Irving Howe believed that *Zelig* "reflected Jewish experience" in America. Saul Bellow believed that in Zelig's sickness was "the root of his salvation."

Clever and witty on the surface, *Zelig* also suggests, more seriously, some of the crucial aspects of the fictive personality: its emptiness, its narcissistic strivings, its limitless need for unconditional love, its potential violence (Zelig joins the Nazis), and its instability and capacity for deception.

Allen's portrait as it is manifested in a woman in *The Purple Rose of Cairo* is much more gentle and warm-hearted. During the Great Depression, Cecilia works as a waitress in a diner with her sister, but her "real" emotional life is attached to romantic movies and intimate stories about the stars. She certainly does not have an easy life. By day her out-of-work husband pitches pennies and hangs out with cronies; at night he guzzles beer and occasionally beats Cecilia. She goes to see a highly romantic film called *The Purple Rose of Cairo* in which one of her favorite actors, Gil Shepard, plays Tom Baxter, an explorer and poet. More and more wrapped up in the fantasy of the film, she makes a mess at work and is fired. Aimlessly, she wanders toward home and on the way stops in the movie theater, where she spends the day. After seeing the movie for the fifth time, she becomes so intensely engaged in the film romance and so distant from her disappointing reality that she suddenly "sees" Tom Baxter looking at her from the screen. "My God," he says (or seems to say), "you must really love this picture. . . . I've got to speak to you." He steps out from the screen and walks into the theater, explaining to her that whereas she, a real person, wants to be in films, he wishes to be in real life. Sharing opposite wishes yet identical aims, Cecilia and Tom run away together. Later, to complicate matters, Cecilia meets Gil Shepard, the real actor who played Tom Baxter, and the character Tom and actor Gil vie for her affections. The actor tells her:

> "He's fictional. Tell him you can't love him. Do you want to waste your life with a fictional character?"
> "I can learn to be real," Tom says.
> "You can't learn to be real. . . . Some of us are real and some are not."

Gil is right; but the reverse isn't true. Cecilia, like Zelig, is learning to be a fictional character. At last, in her fantasies, she walks into the screen and joins the cast of the movie. There, the actors claim that *they* are real—the audience is a dream. "I've just met a wonderful new man," Cecilia says. "He's fictional, but you can't have everything." Cecilia's unhappiness, her economic and physical brutalization, and the pointlessness of her life pull her inside her fantasies, and the audience is obliged to experience them with her. At the end of the film, we see her sitting in the motion-picture theater, beginning to get involved in a new film, and slightly smiling.

In the male-oriented *Zelig*, the main character searches actively for a self; the function of others, including that of his female analyst, is to offer him models by which, through emulation, he can achieve identity. In the second film, Cecilia is portrayed as a much more passive, inner-oriented person who sits and waits for fantasies to drift over her. Zelig gets his fictive personalities in society, Cecilia gets hers from her internalized participation in the fantasies of others—gossip, magazines, films, actors, actresses. Her emphasis is on loving others, having someone worthy of love, rather than, in the case of Zelig, getting love, which is more typical of the male orientation.

Male, female, child, adult, gambler, lover, soldier—countless are the roles assumed by the fictive personality in novels, plays, and films.

# 5

# Living Fictions

The psychoanalyst Humberto Nagera once reported a case in connection with his studies of female sexuality and the Oedipus complex in which a young woman patient indicated that if he wanted to understand her, he should make a thorough study of Émile Zola's novel *Nana*. The young woman—"Miss Q," Nagera calls her—explains that the heroine of this book is a prostitute and has had many lovers. Among these, the one that stands out for Miss Q is a count, a pious man married to a cold, puritanical woman. His meeting with Nana has changed the count completely. He realizes that she is superior to his rigid wife, and he feels genuine passion for her, such as he has never felt for the countess. He becomes mad to possess her, Miss

Q says exultantly; he would do anything to have her. Miss Q concludes that she *is* Nana. She wishes to be a prostitute too. "Nana is very kind, you know, even if she is a prostitute," Miss Q maintains. She uses the present tense in speaking of Nana because for Miss Q Nana is not dead, nor is she a character in a novel. She is alive in the present—in Miss Q's identification with her.

The case of Miss Q is a relatively simple example of how fictive personality processes may fuse with developmental issues, such as the Oedipus complex. When Oedipal yearnings cannot be fulfilled in reality, they may seem gratified through identification with a fiction. Two cases, both considerably more complicated, show how the self strives—through fictions, if need be—to complete its developmental tasks.

The first concerns Arthur, a young New Yorker who moved from a basic fictive orientation toward creative production as a writer by using his own experience of himself as a model. Arthur began psychoanalytic treatment at the age of twenty-one, after graduation from a midwestern college. He seemed to relish telling the tale that was his life. Soon it became evident that everyone in his life, as he saw it, was playing someone else's part. His businessman father was a tough-talking, hard-bitten New York con man, a Ring Lardner or Damon Runyon kind of character. His mother emerged in his stories as a bright, attractive, but brittle woman, romantic but plucky—sometimes playing Merle Oberon roles, at other times those of Bette Davis. He tended to see himself as a cross between Heathcliff and an F. Scott Fitzgerald character. When asked about these identifications, he responded readily, and gave elaborately detailed, obsessive descriptions of the precise ways in which these roles were "exactly the truth."

Behind these fictions lay the truth that Arthur was at war with his father and adored his mother. In loud arguments he accused his father of having no sensitivity. His father in turn accused him of being irresponsible and complained that Arthur still acted as if he were in a playpen. But, as Arthur claimed, how could Nathan Detroit appreciate Heathcliff? In contrast, he was extremely attached to his mother. As late as his high-school years, he spent several afternoons each week lying with his mother in her bed, holding hands while they watched television. Everything about his relationship to her was romanticized.

She treated him in similar fashion. Many times she told him that a great destiny lay in store for him. She promised that he would achieve greatness and glory as an artist; Arthur's fame would put his father to shame. With her help, Arthur embraced the myth of the artist hero. He felt alienated? The true artist was always outside his society! He felt unrecognized? That was often the early experience of the romantic artist, too special a person to be understood at once! He felt critical of his businessman father? It was right for an artist to attack commercial middle-class values! He loved his mother, but couldn't have her? Unrequited love was the perfect inspiration for an artist! It all fit. No less than Don Quixote, Arthur had formulated a self from the romantic myths about the artist. This myth made it seem as if all his failures and angers and struggles with his father were evidence of greatness to come.

Arthur's entire emotional life thus came under the sway of fictions. He could not experience "life" unless he could find a fictional model to correspond with a person or occurrence. If he felt depressed, he would say, "I'm Josef K., my world is Kafka's." Or he would pose and gesture and describe himself as "a Chekhov character." When he felt passive, he'd say, "Here I am, Oblomov again," and he'd stay in bed for long periods just like Goncharov's character.

In his mind, he pictured a grand building containing busts of great writers, a Literary Hall of Fame. He visualized his own marble bust among those of Tolstoy, Melville, Flaubert, and Dickens—all nineteenth-century writers. In this vision, he assured himself that his mother was right after all—immortality was his destiny.

Not surprisingly, behind this vision was the profound fear that he might, instead, be a child and a fake, just as his father had said. To protect himself, Arthur developed identifications with literary characters who proved their fathers to be fakes or who won out over their fathers. Sometimes he saw himself as Huckleberry Finn, whose father was a vulgar drunk; at others, he was Alyosha in *The Brothers Karamazov*. Most often he saw himself as Jay Gatsby, his real origins (like Gatsby's) hidden in obscurity. "How could that man be my father?" Arthur would say about his own father.

Arthur was a young man whose self-esteem was so fragile that in times of stress he had to see himself through others' fictions, or he might not have been able to see himself at all. At the same time, the variety of his identifications and the generally high level of his choices suggests that he was well-read, intelligent, and sensitive.

These qualities saved him from being simply a composite of fictions—these, and a lucky break! During a summer session, he took a writing class from a well-respected screenwriter. Arthur's needs, and probably his basic talent, must have impressed or appealed to the writer, and he gave Arthur extra attention. After the class, Arthur continued to see his teacher, and with this writer's help Arthur was allowed to participate in an advanced film-writing program.

Following this, Arthur actually began to write, instead of dreaming about being a writer. Arthur's mentor recommended several contemporary books to him, and Arthur soon began to give up his rivalry with the nineteenth-century classics, even as his competitive feelings toward his father lessened through analysis.

Among the writers who then attracted Arthur's attention was the Japanese novelist and screenwriter Yukio Mishima. No wonder. Mishima was and is one of those writers who evokes either great admiration or scorn. As the author of

*The Sailor Who Fell from Grace with the Sea* and many other books, Mishima was deeply conflicted about whether his main identification was with the West, the new, and art, or with Japan, tradition, and politics. Moving from the first set of values to the second, he organized a proto-fascist private army modeled on the samurai code, and attempted to return Japan to its seventeenth-century traditions. Frustrated in his aims, he committed hara-kiri in the ritual Japanese manner.

Arthur's identification was primarily with Mishima as a writer. But, some of his own ambivalence and suppressed anger showed through in his choice of Mishima as a model. Sometimes Arthur felt that he too should strike a blow against the shallowness of modern society, as Mishima had tried to do; at other times, when depression seized him, he felt, like Mishima, that there was no alternative to suicide.

At around the same time, Arthur also began to study contemporary film criticism; he admired the writings of Paul Schrader, the screenwriter who had written *Taxi Driver*. Naturally and easily, he passed from interest in Schrader's criticism to a close study of his films. Things clicked for him when he learned that Schrader's first film was about Japan and that its subject was the Japanese underworld of gangsters. Its title was *Yakuza*. Eventually the film was shown in his city, and Arthur rushed to see it. The film concerns an American who returns to Japan years after army service in World War II and its aftermath in the occupation of Japan, and how he becomes involved in the violent, ritualistic Japanese criminal world. There is a shocking conclusion in which the American, completely attuned to the Japanese vision of honor, follows Yakuza tradition by cutting off one of his fingers to expiate an instance of dishonor. It does not take much analytic subtlety to see that in his fantasies about Mishima and about the criminal underworld, Arthur was attempting, at considerable remove, to make some rapprochement with his (as he saw it) distant, cruel, criminal father.

Arthur's identifications both with Mishima and Paul Schrader deepened. At one level, this was natural, since Arthur himself was writing screenplays. From another perspective, Schrader had done just what Arthur wanted to do. Arthur became fascinated with the details of Schrader's life and activities and ideas. He said that he had had "the very thoughts" that Schrader had put into the mouths of Travis Bickle and the main character of *Yakuza*—played by Robert Mitchum. From a loose melange of gossip and reportage in magazines and interviews, Arthur came to the conclusion that Schrader and he were much alike. Schrader, he reported, had a history of violent acts, kept a gun by his bedside, was brooding and temperamental. Arthur said he had read that Schrader had had a Calvinist upbringing, a strict, moralistic father, and that he confessed to a fantasy that he should blow his bad thoughts out of his head with a gun. Arthur even claimed that Schrader was just as interested as he was in Mishima.

It is likely that Arthur had read somewhere about Schrader's interest in Mishima, though he claimed simply to "know" it. Possibly, however, he made a leap of understanding, at the unconscious level, out of his identification with both Schrader and Mishima. In any event, Arthur was right: soon it was public knowledge that Schrader was writing a film about Mishima's life.

Two things helped Arthur to make something potentially creative out of these equally potentially dangerous identifications. One was his friendship with the older writer, who became (in Arthur's eyes) like a "second father." The other was that his fascination and identification with Mishima and Schrader were worked through in analysis. They were explored even as they arose and therefore never had a chance to get "stuck" as false selves in his psyche.

At the end of this phase of the analysis, then, rather than

being molded by them, Arthur used his fictive identifications for his own growth. They helped him toward his own creative productions. What remained of his identification with Schrader after its aggressive aspects had been analyzed was a good model: Schrader as a competent, professional writer of screenplays. Now Arthur also saw Mishima as a writer of brilliance, from whom he could learn a great deal, but his interest in Mishima's darker aspects diminished.

A second case, also involving a writer, shows in another way the complications that can result from fictive identifications. This patient, Thomas, grew up in a southwestern state as the only child of strict, fundamentalist parents. His father, an evangelist preacher, was often away on church business, leaving Thomas alone with his mother. The family subscribed to the belief that bad thoughts were equivalent to bad deeds: "If thine eye offend thee, pluck it out." According to his mother, Thomas's father was a "saint," and his mother wanted Thomas to be a "saint" too. During his childhood, he had to be "just like your father and, of course, just like Christ." "I had to be what my mother wanted me to be," Thomas said. So far as he knew, this was the way everyone was: one part of you—"the sinful part, the wild part, the part that didn't want to do your duty"—had to stay hidden, while the other "good boy" part had to seem like his own identity.

Highly skilled with language—again, like his father—and frequently praised by his teachers for his excellent compositions, Thomas seemed destined to be a writer. He wrote without mistakes; his sentiments and ideas, if conventional, were high-minded; and he took up austere and moral topics. Even his penmanship was perfect. Eventually, after graduate school in English he found himself writing literary criticism. His standards were high, his judgments severe, his analysis meticulous. He wrote prolifically. If he did not complete an article for each Sunday of the year, as did his father with sermons, he nonetheless seemed a marvel of productivity to all his colleagues. In addition to countless articles, books, and public lectures, he wrote poems and stories distinguished by their seriousness and high quality of craftsmanship. He published in literary journals and small quarterlies. When Thomas was in his early thirties, his father died; but Thomas continued to play at being his father, for his mother's sake. He had married and was the father of one child.

His literary interests, which ranged widely but centered in literary modernism, led him to a study of several authors whose works included substantial components of sexual and even perverse materials. Thomas saw in this no conflict with his background, and justified it as a part of a serious interest in a particular literary movement.

What became quite clear, however, was that these authors were expressing feelings and ideas close to what Thomas had always relegated to his private, hidden self. Thomas could not acknowledge this, of course, even to himself, but his intensive reading helped to bring this hidden being closer to the surface.

As an experiment—so he told himself—Thomas decided to try "automatic writing," a technique developed by the surrealists to bring forth unconscious materials. Late at night, when his defenses and inhibitions were eroded by a hard day's work, Thomas darkened his room, tried to relax, then wrote down whatever came into his mind. Soon he formed a plan—which he elaborately disguised and rationalized to himself—to write a popular novel charged with sexual content in a futuristic setting. Later he said that when he let his mind go, the exotic and erotic scenes and episodes drifted, it almost seemed, before his eyes, as if the characters and settings displaced the features of his own room.

His first novel was accepted by a reputable publisher, and rapidly he wrote others. He did not list these books on his *curriculum vitae* when he submitted his annual review at the university where he taught, but he took a secret satisfaction at seeing these popular, risqué books arranged alphabetically under his name in *Books in Print*, and also when he saw them on the shelves in the university bookstore, where, he presumed, they sold better than his scholarly works.

Then one day he received a letter from his mother, who had seen one of his novels in a bookstore and had bought it. She couldn't believe he had written it, yet it had his name on it. And a few of the details and turns of phrase had convinced her, contrary to everything she wanted to believe, that he was indeed the author. "If you did write that book," she said, "you must have been out of your mind when you did it. How could you let yourself even think such things?" There followed considerable advice about the dangers of insulating oneself in a university life, where few morals existed; admonitions about the bad influence of fiction; reminders of how his father would react were he alive; and advice about prayer and taking a "true path" back to God.

Thomas reacted with unexpected calmness. His mother, he told himself, was narrow-minded. He consoled himself that Joyce and Yeats, Cendrars, Lawrence, and Breton would have approved of his work. But he had trouble getting his next book started. When he did "indulge" in fantasy now, he became convinced that he would have to act out the sexual scenes or adventures he conjured up. He felt as if he would be compelled to leave his wife. He thought a good deal about having sex with his students; he had fantasies about injuring, even killing, himself. Depressed, he stopped working altogether: his prolific creativity suddenly ceased.

In modeling his life on the parts his mother had given him to play, Thomas had split himself, forcing his instinctual drives into hiding. His life consisted of two fictions: the false public self and the hidden secret self. His writing of the novels constituted a restorative wish to ally the secret with the public self, to bring his split self together; his mother

was right that his success and the more permissive environment of the university had encouraged him to make the
empt at being whole. But his mother's letter had shattered
reasserting forcefully what he had been taught as a
that bad thoughts led to bad actions. Her letter said,
nce, that his hidden self was a crazy, sinful being
ld be rooted out.

helped to provide a new forum by which Thomas
make the attempt at self-integration. Encouraged
mas at first refused to lie down; but he did
te freely and to say whatever came into his
between his associations and his superego
inhibitions soon followed: he should not
nd such a thought, the analyst would
im out of treatment, think ill of him,
might add defensively, his thoughts
was a good person, his thoughts
a little voice inside him, and so
he argued, should be to get these
ctually helped him to associate
nside him could be emptied
and over he had to be told
acceptable to the analyst;
be obliged to act upon
analyst was deceiving
m to regard his hidden
k him after he had
pated attack didn't
ing out more and
egan to feel like

ll kinds, had
experimen-
ion of his
it-off self.

When these two selves were linked, he seemed to lose the drives that had produced his writing—a kind of secular preaching, or anti-preaching—and he was now generally content with his life and family except for the fact that he was no longer writing. This left him depressed, since authorship, at the level of the ego, had become a part of his self-esteem. After a "dry" period, he began writing again—but not nearly so compulsively—in an interdisciplinary field that incorporated and fused together most of the elements of his previously divided interests.

In what way do authors identify with the characters th create? Or, to put it another way, how do characters ref the author? Freud took up these questions in his best-kn essay on literary productions, "Creative Writers and Dreaming," of 1908. At the end of his essay he com on the egocentric aspect of literary creation. "One above all cannot fail to strike us about the creations story writers," he remarks. "Each of them has a h is the centre of interest, for whom the writer trie our sympathy by every possible means and whom to place under the protection of a special Providen Freud indicates, is not merely literary conventi the very idea of the central hero originally aris importance of preserving the ego. "Through t characteristic of invulnerability," Freud writes mediately recognize His Majesty the Ego, the every day-dream and every story." Freud m distinction between the active aspect of the e in the dynamic hero, and the passive con ego, often appearing as the hero who is a events of the story. Further splitting ma suggests, in assigning different parts of th ego—to various characters, then watchi xternally the same drama that is alwa

Freud's hypotheses were demonstrated in an experiment conducted on the relation between the personality and literary productions in the work of John D. MacDonald, the popular writer of such detective novels as *The Turquoise Lament* and *Darker than Amber*, along with nearly eighty other novels that have sold one hundred million copies worldwide.

The hero of many of MacDonald's novels is a tough detective named Travis McGee. McGee is a white male in his early forties; six feet four inches tall, he has a brawny build. He is physically tough, but hardly invulnerable, since he has suffered a number of injuries, several nearly fatal. He bears many scars. McGee is an expert at killing and is cool under fire. During the Korean War he served as an infantryman, was wounded, and emerged from the war with a Purple Heart and the rank of sergeant. Following the war he became a detective. He operates out of a fifty-two foot houseboat docked in the Fort Lauderdale marina. He describes himself not as a detective but as a "salvage expert" who recovers what people have lost, for one-half its value. Sexually, McGee has been active since age sixteen; he is unmarried. His occupation brings him into frequent contact with women under exciting or tense circumstances, and so it is not surprising that he has had sexual relations with about fifty different women.

McGee's best friend is a semiretired economist named Meyer, who sometimes provides McGee with companionship, sometimes with wisdom, and sometimes with physical or theoretical assistance in his escapades. Meyer is internationally known for his papers on currency exchange and the effects of interest rates on third-world nations. People like him. Meyer is easygoing, rather out of shape, and thoughtful, a calming and cautionary influence upon Travis.

MacDonald has attempted to give what he calls "an illusion of wholeness" through the accumulation of details about Travis and Meyer given out little by little over the whole range of books. In 1986 before his own death, MacDonald announced that the last McGee novel, to be published posthumously, would tell how McGee dies. That he arranged for McGee's death to occur in relation to his own suggests that MacDonald did indeed identify with his hero, and that in investigating MacDonald's personality and biography we should expect to find considerable coincidence with McGee's. (Even the choice of a name similar to his own for his hero suggests this.)

But this expectation is not confirmed. With MacDonald's cooperation, Dr. Raymond D. Fowler, a well-known psychologist, made an interesting experiment. MacDonald had had some previous experience with psychology, having been diagnosed at the Mayo Clinic in 1961 as suffering from acute anxiety, which he treated in self-analysis by reading psychoanalytic literature and by recording and analyzing his dreams. In 1985, at Fowler's suggestion, MacDonald agreed to take a widely used psychological test, the Minnesota Multiphasic Personality Inventory (MMPI). He took it three times, as himself, "as if" he were McGee, and "as if" he were McGee's friend Meyer. Developed over forty years ago, this test is still the most widely used personality profile. More than six thousand studies of the test and its results have been published. After such wide use and study, hundreds of scales and thousands of test patterns have emerged as useful to delineate personality. Since no interpreter could objectively hold in mind all of these patterns, the MMPI has been programmed for computer scoring. The computer produces a narrative report on the personality evidenced by the responses given to 566 statements.

Thus, three computer-generated personality profiles were developed as a result of the three tests taken by MacDonald. The narrative that was produced on the basis of the MMPI taken "as if" he were McGee corresponds precisely to the detective as MacDonald has characterized him in many books:

the computer narrative characterized McGee as "energetic," "easily bored," "impulsive," "risk-taking," "egocentric," "demanding of others in a narcissistic manner," "lacking in adequate conscience development," and therefore "free of inhibiting guilt, anxiety, and remorse"—all characteristics that "fit" McGee very well. Thus, it is clear that MacDonald could consistently "think like" McGee.

MacDonald's personal profile is very different from McGee's. The computer narrative indicated:

> He appears to be a pleasant, friendly, and ambitious person who feels generally happy and effective in life. He is willing to take some risks in life and may show a great deal of initiative. He seems to have a number of plans and is actively pursuing them. He has a rather positive self-image and he seems to be able to deal effectively with other people and to make favorable impressions upon others.
>
> He appears to be happy with life and optimistic about the future. His response content reflects a high degree of self-confidence and the ability to deal with life's tasks. He does not complain of somatic difficulties and considers himself in good health.
>
> He has an average interest in being with others and is not socially isolated or withdrawn. He appears to meet and talk with other people with relative ease and is not overly anxious when in social gatherings.

Indeed, MacDonald and McGee are very nearly opposites.

The computer-produced profile based on the response given by MacDonald when he was thinking "like" Meyer is fascinating. The computer produced a narrative which has several identical paragraphs to those in MacDonald's own profile. The only differences are those derived from age: Meyer is in his 50s, while MacDonald was 70 when he took the test. Fowler concluded:

> McGee is a creature of MacDonald's imagination who has almost no similarities to MacDonald in personality, behavior

or life-style. Meyer, on the other hand, could well be called MacDonald's alter ego. Intelligent and thoughtful, with a great store of information and ability to stand back and consider before acting, Meyer plays a vital role for McGee and perhaps for MacDonald as well. Meyer provides MacDonald with an opportunity to enter McGee's life, to talk with him, advise him and react to him. Although McGee is the narrator, it is through the eyes of Meyer, and therefore MacDonald, that we see Travis McGee's world.

William Butler Yeats once described his concept of the "mask" as that which was opposite to one's identity but identical with his desire. Travis McGee seems to be this precisely— MacDonald's "mask," the fiction of his creator's desire. Meyer is MacDonald's identity in fiction. But McGee is his fictive identity.

Each in his own way—Arthur, Thomas, and John D. MacDonald—used fiction to explore, and in some manner to solve, problems of identity. Actors and actresses, as we shall see, take an even more varied route to exploring identity in the roles they play.

# 6

# "Will the Real Paul Newman Please Stand Up?"

**P**aul Newman, like many other people in the acting profession, has occasionally complained that his audience mistakes his own personality for the roles he plays. Newman, for instance, has been often cast as a tough but sexy guy. "The thing I resent about this sex symbol thing," he told an interviewer recently, "is that writers create these . . . flamboyant, aggressive characters who might have nothing to do with who you are under the skin. You don't always have Tennessee Williams around to write glorious lines for you."

However, Newman—again, like many others in his profession—has not been entirely free of the confusion he complains about in others. When he was playing high livers like Hud or Fast Eddie, he notes, he'd wake up feeling hung-over. "You get to the point," he says, "where it's much easier to play a role that has been examined and accepted on the screen than it is to play yourself." He acknowledges that off-stage he adopted mannerisms of the characters he was playing on the screen. "You have such an investment in the roles you play," Newman notes. "You have to step back sometimes and figure out whether you're doing you or somebody else. Will the real Dustin Hoffman please stand up? Where is Jack Nicholson? Where is Marlon 'I could have been a contender' Brando?" In 1986 Newman told an interviewer: "That would be a good title for your article—'Will the Real Paul Newman Please Stand Up?' "

By profession, actors and actresses must learn to play parts, shift shapes, take on roles. As far back as Plato's dialogue with the actor Ion, we know, the best players were able to fuse their personalities with their roles, so that the identity of person and role, not the gap between them, shone forth.

Undoubtedly, a major influence upon the frequency, if not predominance, of fictive personality in the modern acting profession is related to the influence of the great theoretician of acting, Constantin Stanislavski. Again and again in his book *An Actor Prepares* and elsewhere, Stanislavski returned to the same theme, that an actor should "feel the situation of the person in a part so keenly . . . [that] he actually puts himself in the place of that person." His insistence on confusing and fusing actor and role as well as character and person is fundamental to his method. When the actor finds his way into a role, Stanislavski writes, he "ceases to act, he begins to live the life of the play . . . and some of the sensations of the character you portray come very close to your own." The actor's "I Am," unlike Descartes', means: "I have put myself into the very center of imaginary circumstances . . . I exist as the heart of an imaginary life, in a world of imaginary things."

"For method acting," a recent critic has written, "*becoming the character* was the whole point." The Stanislavski method has been enormously influential, not only through his personal influence, or through his writing, but also because of his powerful effect on several disciples who have spread method acting to theaters everywhere in the West. Only in the late 1980s is method acting being challenged.

Are persons who become actors or actresses influenced psychologically by the continuous emphasis on becoming the parts they play in their profession? And does this bring them strongly into the sphere of the fictive personality? Or, are people (like Vonnegut's Harry) who have some prior pleasurable contact with fictive processes drawn especially toward certain professions, such as acting? The answer would seem to be yes to all the questions.

It seems equally evident that there is as wide a variation among actors in their susceptibility to fictions as there is in the other professions. I suppose that when he emerged from his rhapsody, Plato's Ion resumed normal activities. Actors and actresses share in the ordinary activities of the rest of the populace; they may belong to organizations, raise children, join political groups, cook dinners, clear brush, or run for political office. That is to say, most actors assume roles temporarily, provisionally, with a suspension of disbelief, and only in a "sealed-off," trained part of consciousness.

Still, the impression persists that some players seek parts to play because they have little integrative power to create an identity of their own, and that other actors and actresses tap a special reservoir in the act and art of taking roles. Nathanael West, in his novel *The Day of the Locust*, described the first kind of player in characterizing a young actress named Faye Greener. Left alone, he says, Faye soon began to seek out fantasies through which to come alive. She had a fairly fixed set of fantasies to which she returned over and over again; West compared them to a deck of cards. Shuffling through her mental deck, she would choose a fantasy card that struck her fancy at the moment, and then "live" in her fiction as long as possible.

She would get some music on the radio, then lie on her bed and shut her eyes. She had a large assortment of stories to choose from. After getting herself in the right mood, she would go over them in her mind, as though they were a pack of cards, discarding one after another until she found the one that suited. On some days, she would run through the whole pack without making a choice. When that happened, she would either go to Vine Street for an ice cream soda or, if she was broke, thumb over the pack again and force herself to choose.

While she admitted that her method was too mechanical for the best results and that it was better to slip into a dream naturally, she said that any dream was better than no dream and beggars couldn't be choosers.

One fantasy was really as good as another: any one would do, so long as it was a good fiction.

Faye, however, is a "bit" player, an extra. She resembles the schizoid young woman who told the psychiatrist R. D. Laing that she could become anyone, anytime, anywhere: "I'm Rita Hayworth, I'm Joan Blondell. I'm a Royal Queen." Very likely, the most convincing actors and actresses fall into the category of players who are able to discover in themselves powerful processes that can be fused with a role to create persuasive impersonations.

It may be useful to illustrate briefly the varied presence of these processes in actors and actresses, beginning in the nineteenth century. So far as we can tell, William Cody lived a life that was normal for a frontier scout until 1869, when the "dime novelist" and playwright Ned Buntline found him sleeping under a wagon and began to write about him as Buffalo Bill. Having become something of a celebrity through Buntline's works, Cody visited Chicago in 1872. Here, his career had a turning point. He was offered $500 a week "to play the part of Buffalo Bill myself," "to represent my own character," he writes in his autobiography. "I feared I would be a total failure," he wrote. But eventually he did go on stage, and so began the remarkable transformation of Cody into "Buffalo Bill." This unlettered plainsman, under the impact of the fictions he imitated, developed into a sophisticated, courtly hero. More and more he looked like General Custer. Eventually, in his Wild West Show, he "fought," with fake bullets and blunted arrows, the Indians he had once actually battled. By the end, he no longer seemed to know the difference, and in his old age when he wrote his autobiography, its hero was the fictional character invented long before by Buntline.

In 1979, an updated version of the same story made news. After decades of playing the Lone Ranger on radio and television, in films and circuses, Clayton Moore was obliged by the copyright owners to give up the part in favor of a younger replacement. He refused. He would not remove his mask— until at last a court decision forced him to drop his mask and, presumably, reassume his "real" identity. But the Lone Ranger, he claimed, had become his true identity, displacing the original self. Wearing a mask-like pair of dark sunglasses, Moore began to appeal to his audience to give him back his self. To crowds he told the story of "his" life with such an air of reality that one bystander was led to remark: "This guy really thinks he's the Lone Ranger." Moore himself says that he "fell in love" with the character and "it helped to make a better person of me . . . I tell the truth [according to] the Lone Ranger creed."

Several contemporary actresses seem to operate out of a similarly deep engagement. Maggie Smith has been quoted as saying, "You don't feel alive unless you have a part to act. It's structured, and that gives you the feeling of really living." Elizabeth Taylor's stepson, Michael Todd, Jr., speculated that his father and Taylor's marriage would have endured had Michael senior not been killed, because, "As for

Elizabeth, she can play any role she's given. And she loved the role she played with my father. It was just about the time of his death that her marriage was no longer a role. It became her personality and her life."

In an interview in 1984, Sally Field was able to define more deeply the place that fictions had in her early life and the way this experience pushed her toward the theater. Her early years, she has said, were filled with uncertainty and anxiety:

> "My childhood was not terrific," she said. "I was raised at the tail end of the ladylike era when you were supposed to look a certain way and act a certain way so as to please others. Your own feelings didn't count.
> "I was told to behave myself and not be ugly. I was rewarded for being a good little girl and not causing problems. . . ."

Field was taught to become whatever was wanted of her. "I was raised to sense what someone wanted me to be and be that kind of person. It took me a long time to not judge myself through someone else's eyes." Her mother's remarriage presented Sally with particularly confusing problems.

> "I was always anxious around my stepfather. I felt as if I had to put on a show all the time. I just learned to stop pretending to be a good little girl last year," she says, laughing. "My mother always told me to listen to a man, ask him about himself, and laugh at his jokes."

Acting gave her a solution, a way of expressing her bound-up feelings. "I found out that you could act as crazy as you felt, let out all your feelings and get applause for it. What a revelation! But even while I was learning how to release my emotions in a safe way, I still couldn't handle them personally."

Many actors and actresses, of course, have entered therapy; in their treatment, major issues usually revolve around narcissistic losses, such as those described by Sally Field, leading to a weakened sense of self, or to a belief that it is necessary to hide the true self behind a mask, acting out false roles—false selves—as a way of disguising (but partly revealing indirectly) feelings and thoughts that seem best left hidden.

Again, it is important to remember that, in its origin, this is a very normal process. All children love to play roles, roles they create themselves or ones derived from the media. "Let's play! Let's pretend!" Or they don't even pretend. For a moment they *are* the roles they play—they have no trouble at all being other people. Laurence Olivier speaks of the fictive sense as being "kept active by novels, movies, and various other invented lives," and suggests that this sort of play allows us to have, in an imaginary sense, the lives "we once could have reached." He says that especially in acting we live out the lives we dream about, "the futures we are not likely to have."

Olivier tells us something about himself in this comment, as well as something about fantasy and the motivations that lead people into acting. Resembling Sally Field's reasons more closely than Olivier's, an actress whom I shall call Andrea helps to add to my picture. Andrea has been in analysis for many years, and has come to regard psychoanalysis as helpful and even necessary to acting. As a child she led a lonely life. She was convinced that her mother cared nothing about her, having exhausted her capacity for affection on three older female children. Her father traveled extensively and seldom had time for Andrea when he was home. Andrea's earliest memory was of her mother and father leaving for a trip to the Orient when she was four. Years later she still felt that they were cruel and heartless to do this to her. At school she had difficulty in making friends. She dreamed of being the center of attention, and all through childhood and adolescence she acted out and acted up in many different ways. Without exactly intending to do so, she drifted into the movie industry. Others in the business pushed her along because they assumed that she wanted to act, for she was good-looking and skilled at improvising roles. But they were wrong. She actually had little interest in acting itself. She didn't want to act, but she very much wanted to be a star.

In this sense, and only in this sense, Andrea valued her beauty, because to be a star, as she saw it, one had to be beautiful. Still, she was haunted by fears that her beauty would fade, that "her kind of look" would fall out of fashion, that she would age badly or too quickly.

All her hurts, fears, and compulsions dropped away when she was acting, however. She deliberately sought work in serial shows in order to have a continuous role. "I feel panic when I am not working," she said, "just sort of dead. That's why I like the series I'm on, because it's very hard work, you hardly have time to do anything else, you just work, work, work. And it will probably go on for years."

More important than the need to work continuously to stave off panic, Andrea acts because *being a star* is her identity, her role in life. The role she really values involves concern with everyone on the set. She "mothers" everyone, but underneath that she is doing everything she can to win her private audience—the production crew and fellow actors. She doesn't care as much about the public audience of millions whom she will never see as she does about the several dozen people producing the show every day. In analysis she explained: "There are important things you have to do when you are a star. You have to see that things are done right on the set. You have to see that everyone is in the proper place; you have to come on time. You have to be kind to the workers; you have to see that the catering is being done correctly. You are the star, and you have to set the right tone." Clearly she achieved the center of attention that she wanted to have by taking care of everyone else, and by being the provider of benefits for the whole crew—a good mother and father to everyone, and therefore admired by everyone.

Between jobs, analysis often became a holding action, a container to keep Andrea together. In one session she revealed: "Every once in awhile I wake up in the middle of the night and I am terrified and I am not sure who I am. I get so frightened that I sort of crawl around on the floor and whimper. It's like being helpless and like a little animal. I don't know why this happens but I have the feeling that I don't know who I am at that time. At other times I know who I am and I am successful and appear on a TV series and people know me and I like that feeling."

Other movie or television stars, of course, lead "normal" lives between films, but find special opportunities in certain parts. One of the recurring observations about Meryl Streep concerns her ability to change considerably with her roles— to convey a new aura of personality with each part. The only thing she is passionately demanding about, she has said of herself, is her work: "I can be as demanding within the boundaries of fiction as I want," she remarks. "Her approach," David Rosenthal wrote, ". . . is simply to assume the life of whomever it is she is about to portray. To become part of the landscape, as Meryl aptly puts it, to see a character's world and simply step right in. To disappear into the warped reality of acting fiction and emerge as someone else. To do so too well can be scary."

Karel Reisz, the director of *The French Lieutenant's Woman*, observed that Streep is "liberated" by costumes. Accepting the British Academy Award for her role in *The French Lieutenant's Woman*, she said: "Call me in six years and the character will still be inside me. Usually it's difficult to get inside a character; this one is difficult to get out of." No costumes were necessary when she played Sophie in the film of William Styron's novel *Sophie's Choice;* but to prepare for the part Streep spent five months getting a linguistic costume—learning Polish. Everyone involved in the film, according to reports, was astonished "when, at the first reading around the table, Streep looked up to speak and it was Sophie who spoke. It was as if, [Alan] Pakula says, 'Meryl Streep had ceased to exist.'" During breaks on the set she continued, in conversation, to speak with a Polish accent.

However, the performer who most clearly "acted" in order to exist as a "person" is Peter Sellers. Peter Sellers was the son of an actress and a piano player. He was their second child, but the first, also a boy, had died soon after birth, even before being named. Peter was destined to take his place, and from the first he lived out the role of the dead sibling. He was petted and spoiled; his mother, Peg, would not allow anyone to discipline him or to criticize him. Yet she herself was a basically cold, self-absorbed woman. She was back on stage a week after Peter was born. On the one hand, she was indulgent; on the other, she was distant and badly neglected her child. While she rehearsed and performed, she kept the infant in a basket in the wings, and as a result he contracted bronchial pneumonia. When she did show him attention, it was as an extension of herself. When he was three weeks old she had him carried onto the stage while the audience was asked to sing a chorus of "For He's a Jolly Good Fellow" in his honor. By the time he reached two and a half, she had a suit of white tie, top hat, and tails made for him and brought him into the act, where he sang "My Old Dutch." This early he showed the petulance that would develop in his adult years. He hated to be exhibited, and once he threw down his top hat and stamped on it.

The portrait of Sellers that emerges in Alexander Walker's biography is of a child whose mother treated him as a transitional object: at one and the same time, she didn't see him as sufficiently separate from her, while she also dropped him entirely when it suited her. In short, he was to play roles for and at her pleasure—but she became an audience only when she wished to be.

Sellers began to play roles for others as a natural extension of the role-playing into which his mother had forced him. He became an irrepressible and brilliant mimic, and he used these talents to earn love or attention. In later years he recalled that when he was thirteen years old he wanted to gain the favors of a girl his age. The way he tried to do so showed that he believed he could be loved only as a fiction. "I found that she had a movie hero," he recalled. "Errol Flynn. I'd seen him in *The Dawn Patrol*, and that was good enough. The next day I put on his voice, his accent, his mannerisms. I even threw in a background of airplane and machine-gun noises for good measure." He became an imitation of the whole movie—but it didn't work. Later, the girl became a fan of Robert Donat's. "So I went to any Donat films I could find playing . . . and went through the whole act again with his voice. No luck this time, either."

A few years later he was still following the same mode of playacting to get affection. When he was seventeen he "put on a trench coat, the kind Bogart was wearing in the gangster movies, a trilby [soft felt hat] like William Powell's and a Clark Gable mustache." He threw in a syrupy Robert Donat voice for good measure. He was now becoming a collage of fictions. He played at being a talent scout and "auditioned" the local girls. "I enjoyed the impersonations," he said, "for the feeling of power it gave me. Nobody paid that kind of attention to plain Peter Sellers." For the most part, he didn't even identify with actual people, only with the parts played by actors. He was a fiction derived from fictions.

As a result, Sellers remained fixated at an extremely vulnerable stage of development. Even toward the end of his life, when he was extraordinarily successful, he would moan to his wife whenever he was faced with adult responsibility:

"I'm only a little thing." He had no firm self-regard, and so praise didn't "stick," whereas the slightest hint of criticism would hurt him. If a friend were to say, "Peter, how well you look—you've put on a bit of weight," he would starve himself for days afterward. Good reviews of his acting would be disregarded, but he might clip out a savage review and carry it around with him for weeks. The more successful he was, the more he demanded reassurance. Two film producers with whom he made several films showed in their summaries of his character how much Sellers had burdened them. Said one, "A man with an infinite capacity for sucking people dry"; and the other, "A man of immense dependence seeking ruthlessly, by any means, to establish his independence and preeminence."

Within seconds of being introduced to a role Sellers could bring it to life. He turned mundane characters into remarkable people. He went right into the character so that there seemed to be no question of playing a part.

At the same time, he had trouble getting out of a part. When he was making *I'm All Right, Jack* (1959), the character of Kite stayed with him when the company broke for lunch. Around this time, he himself began to speak of having "weird feelings": he felt that he was being taken over—"possessed," he'd say—by his role. Tirelessly he explained to interviewers that while acting he lived two separate lives, one his own life; the other, the character's. By comparison, his own life was dull. He started to see mediums to help him make decisions. He felt that he was possessed by spirits the way a medium is; they were struggling to get at him, to seize hold of him. In order to explain this to himself—for he never lost the logic of reality-testing—he decided that these spirits must be attached to lives that he had led in the remote past. He began, in fact, to claim, as he told an interviewer for the *Evening Standard*, that "there's no such person as Peter Sellers. . . . I have no personality as such of my

own. . . . I can't move. I can't talk. . . . I only exist as
the various characters I create. They are more than me."

Between films he lapsed into a sort of dazed nonexistence,
trying to keep alive through expensive toys or social images.
He was ready to adopt almost any role offered to him. Once,
when a minor Indian actress came up to him and said she
thought he "was the new messiah," Sellers instantly responded internally to the new, grandiose role: "I even began
to feel I had developed the power to heal people. . . ."
Many actors make a film every two years. In 1962, Peter
Sellers made six; between 1958 and 1968, twenty-nine of
his films appeared. Even when he suffered a series of heart
attacks, he couldn't stop working: either way he faced death.
The loss of a self, or the loss of life—what was the difference?

A special version of theater in contemporary arts is the
mixture of drama and fine art in what has come to be known
as "performance art." In this genre, the performer makes
an art of his actions. While such art had its formal origin
in inimitable, unique "happenings," such as those designed
by Allen Kaprow, some artists have developed small reper-
toires of performances that they can and do repeat for different
audiences. It is not surprising that performance art draws
so fundamentally upon fictive processes that "performance"
and fictive personality can become indistinguishable. A performance artist does not masquerade, but instead gives a
"real-life performance."

In the fall of 1980, the performance artist Eleanor Antin
decided to "become" Eleanora Antinova. She first invented
Antinova, then she became her invention; but in order to
become Antinova, she had to write a history and a playing
script for her. Her scenario for Antinova's creation was her
diary, in turn, of how she became Antinova. As her invention
grew, Antinova grew into "being" a black ballerina who
had for a time during the 1920s performed with Diaghilev's

Ballet Russe de Monte Carlo. Now having outlived most
of the company, she decides to visit New York City. There
she will put a notice in the paper inviting old colleagues,
friends, and admirers of the company (along with an invited
group of critics and viewers known to be interested in performance art) to a gallery and studio theater for a few afternoons
and evenings of conversation about the old days. Her fiction
is that, like Zelig, she has been forgotten by history.

As invented, Antinova is black; Eleanora Antin had to
spend hours carefully applying black makeup while project-
ing the fiction—even to herself!—that this length of time is
"in line with the time traditionally taken by glamorous women
. . . preparing for the day." From having read in Sono
Ostato's memoirs about the "peaceful morning hours she
was sometimes invited to share with Danilova in her old-
fashioned Monte Carlo suite," Antin understood "what deep
pleasure a glamorous woman gets from these preparations."

All the while, Eleanor Antin is having herself photographed as Eleanora Antinova: walking in blackface around
the streets of New York, having a solitary drink in a café,
chatting with her doorman, and so on. More photographs,
soft-focused stills printed in sepia of Antinova's career in
ballet—Antinova in *L'Esclav*, Antinova in *The Hebrews*, Antinova in *Before the Revolution*—are all assembled in a little
scrapbook-like portfolio and titled *Recollections of My Life with
Diaghilev*. Antin is busy. She gets brown drawing ink and
pens and a brush and does wash drawings of the set designs
that Antinova, had she existed, would have done. Then
she creates the sketchbook that such a person as Antinova
would have drawn—quick, witty sketches: Nijinsky, Picasso,
Isadora Duncan, her fellow dancers, even one of "Myself
at a charity ball at Versailles." She paints life-size masonite
figures to represent other dancers in the ballet she will perform. All these are reproduced, eventually, in her written
and published account—itself another performance—of her

restoration of Antinova's life—a life of a person Eleanor Antin became.

Inevitably, of course, history had to collide with fiction. There are, after all, former members of the Ballet Russe still living in New York City, and an advertisement in *The New York Times* stating that Eleanora Antinova, formerly of the Monte Carlo troupe, would greet her friends at such and such a gallery caused a stir among the survivors. Discussions were held, and a representative was sent—in search of history, not fiction. Antin recounts that "an elegant old gentleman" entered. He peered closely at the photographs and texts describing the ballets supposedly danced by Antinova. Then, he inquired about the "ballerina." He is introduced to Antin—in blackface. "But you are too young," he says. He seems—for good reason—confused.

> "I am just come from the Tolstoy Farm," he says in a softly modulated British voice. "Spessivtseva lives there."
> He breaks off, unsure of me.
> "Do you know Spessivtseva?"
> "We have been trying to remember you. Later Pat Dolin joined us."
> An ironic smile flits across his mouth.
> "It was Spessivtseva who remembered first. In Spain, she thought. You joined the company in Spain, in Massine's time, Patrick thought it was. In *Las Meninas*. The role of the dwarf. By then he remembered too. Very well. You know Patrick. . . ."
> We share a conspiratorial smile at his friend's expense.
> "It was not a successful ballet, you see. The Spaniards are not an easy people. We thought you might have been of their group when they joined the company.
> It was a little before my time but I too remembered something. . . . Alas, we were wrong."

Antin-Antinova writes in her performance diary that the man was "too old for art"—he didn't understand that she was inventing a dream. All he wanted was history, a renewal of an old acquaintance. She is vaguely resentful that he won't go along with the fiction, as, for instance, the art critic Robert Pincus-Witten did in writing archly (and superciliously) about the performance in *Arts Magazine:* "On taking leave of this grand disastrous wreck of a dancer, one could only grasp those gnarled, but still expressive hands in one's own, raise them to one's lips, bow one's head, and murmur *Toujours la ballerina assolutissima.*"

In the course of her diary, Antin comments that in childhood she had always "dreaded not being noticed," and early on had learned to play the clown, the fool, anything "to catch people's attention," anything not to be "invisible." Unacknowledged for her reality, she could, it seems, only be recognized for her parts. At the end of her three-week performance, she was afraid of not being able to shake off Antinova and resume her own old identity. Was this a pretense as well, a part of her fiction, or did she really experience anxiety? Her book provides no answer, and besides it is in the nature of the performance that no answer should be possible. Did Eleanor Antin dream up Antinova, or is *she* Antinova's dream?

> Did Chouang dream he was a butterfly?
> Or did the butterfly dream Chouang? If so,
> why then all things can change, and change again,
> the sea to brook, the brook to sea, and we
> from man to butterfly; and back to man.

Eleanor Antin gives new meaning to the old riddle of Chuang-tzu's dream.

Antin herself reports a meeting with another performance artist who was looking for a job on Wall Street as an executive trainee so that he could do performances connected with money. " 'But,' " she asks, " 'will they let you quit when the training period is over?' " "He looked surprised. Why would he do that? He wants to work with money, doesn't he? It's his art form. I was impressed. This guy is planning a life performance that might take his whole life." So in performance art, life becomes a performed fiction of a life, without the slightest fissure.

# 7

# Exploring
# The Fictive Personality:
# From Alfred Adler
# to Heinz Kohut

What, then, is this fictive personality that seems a permanent feature of human life, and looms so large in modern times?

Is it a disorder of thought? A deficiency of the self? An emotional disturbance? Does it signify neurosis? Borderline disorder? Psychosis? Is it a compulsion? A choice? Where is its origin—in early disorder and childhood sorrow? In trauma? In the preoedipal stage? In the oedipal stage? Can it be cured? Does it possess value?

Diagnoses do not help understanding here, since diagnoses would apply to a wide spectrum of mental attitudes. Generally speaking, Vonnegut's Harry, Peter Sellers, and John Hinckley all seem to fall into the category of a schizoid disorder, in which there exists only a loose connection between an empty inner self and a vaguely perceived external world. Not everyone would agree. In Hinckley's case, Dr. Carpenter, speaking for the defense, diagnosed Hinckley as suffering from a major depressive disorder and "process schizophrenia," while the government's psychiatric team concluded that he suffered from "dysthymic disorder"—a more mild and transient form of depression—and also from three types of personality disorders: schizoid, narcissistic, and borderline character mixed with passive-aggressive defenses.

As to the others in these pages, one group (Carlos and Melissa) would likely be diagnosed as having "histrionic" or hysterical neuroses. Patty Hearst's personality conversion would most probably be considered as based on her experiences of a sudden trauma and fear of death. The same would be true of the changes in Kristen or other victims of the "Stockholm Syndrome." In contrast, the diagnosis of Mark David Chapman, Travis Bickle, and some others would have to involve some ascription of schizophrenia, internal fragmentation, and paranoia.

Pirandello's Henry IV is spoken of in the play as having "persecution mania" and a "systematized delusion." Yet another group, Terry or Werther, for instance, is marked by evidence of narcissistic deficits—insufficient early mirroring resulting in hollow grandiosity, distorted idealizations, preoccupation with fantasies of unlimited love and public recognition, and a constant yearning for attention. The search for a substitute self, evident in yet another group (Zelig, Miss Q, Don Quixote, and Chapman—seen from another angle) seems to be based on troubles in the area of superego—the need to escape from excessive feelings of shame or inferiority, or from self-punishing guilt feelings by adopting a role in which guilt or shame cannot play a part. When Martin Scorsese says of *Taxi Driver*, "it is almost as if I sat down and wrote a script myself," and when the writer of that script, Paul Schrader, indicates, "I've had a history in my past of violent acts, which I no longer do. One of the stages in stopping them was to be able to do them vicariously in film"—then, both are stressing the paramount importance of their overly harsh superegos. In general, for Scorsese or Schrader becoming another person would also indicate a defense of sublimation. Scorsese put it very directly when he stated that he sees his movies as personal therapy, that he lives in invented lives as a way of venting his own "anger and rage and craziness."

Mild or severe depression, histrionic personality, schizoid processes, schizophrenia, narcissism, trauma, defensiveness, superego problems—these could all be reassigned and ascribed quite differently from what I have done to many of the persons or characters I have mentioned. A compelling argument could be made that with the fictive personality we are always in the area of a special sort of borderline personality, neither neurotic nor psychotic, but a state of widely varied though consistently disordered and distorted emotions. Emptiness, identity confusion, impaired reality testing, suicidal thoughts, repression, grief, rage, and exhibitionistic behavior are the sorts of ascriptions which would be made in the description of fictive personality as the linchpin of the borderline state.

I do not propose to make that argument, however. Instead, I think that fictive personality is involved in the whole range of behavior from normal to psychotic, from thought to emotions, passivity to aggression, creativity to destructiveness. Evidently, the process is a permanent element of human beings. It points to the capacity of people, chameleon-like, to use or be used by fictions, and to take on the costumes and shapes and colors of the psychic environment in which they operate. Fictions are fundamental in dreams, daydreams, aesthetic appreciation, meditations, adaptation, wishes, defense, and many another human impulse. They are a crucial part of the human character, then—the part, especially, that expresses character traits through identification. People say: "I am like Hamlet," "I feel just like Alice in Wonderland," "When I read Portnoy's monologues, it's just like talking to myself," and so on. Identification offers ways: (1) of understanding one's self through comparison to others; (2) of solving problems and facing situations which are perhaps unique to a particular individual, but have, in general terms, been faced many times by others ("All right, I'll have to be a Robinson Crusoe, then!"); (3) of possessing and conveying a special style that others have found useful; (4) or, of learning how to relate to others in a new way. The use of fictions in character development or characteristic behavior is not pathological, and classical psychiatric or diagnostic categories, which start with the concept of pathology and character disorders, cannot give a good account of the nature and operations of fictive processes in character.

A conventional form in classical literature up to the eighteenth century is the literature of character types, as in, say, Plutarch's *Lives* or Thomas Overbury's *Characters*. Recently, Joyce McDougall, in a work titled *Theaters of the Mind*, has proposed what is, in essence, a psychoanalytically informed, updated version of the classical study of character through its typologies or typical manifestations. Her categories are much more varied, of course, than the traditional types, such as "The Brave Soldier," "The Boastful Man," "The Good Wife," and so on. She writes in introducing her topic: " 'All the world's a stage,' and that all the men and women in it are merely players expressed Shakespeare's deep conviction that we do not really escape the roles that are essentially ours. Each of us is drawn into an unfolding life drama in which the plot reveals itself to be uncannily repetitive. Each mind unconsciously shapes itself as a theater or a series of theaters and behavior is directed by the fantasized scenarios of the mind." As McDougall sees the situation, each mind is organized through a variety of internalized "theaters" or dramas. These may be generally harmonious, but they may also result in competing plots, inconsistent scenarios, contradictory conceptions of character, and differing understandings of the world. The mind containing a multitude of "theaters," then, may be harmonized or partly reconciled, or clash and split and break apart.

McDougall says:

> Each of us harbors in our inner universe a number of "characters," parts of ourselves that frequently operate in complete contradiction to one another, causing conflict and mental pain to our conscious selves. For we are relatively unacquainted with these hidden players and their roles. Whether we will it or not, our inner characters are constantly seeking a stage on which to play out their tragedies and comedies. Although we rarely assume responsibility for our secret theater productions, the producer is seated in our own minds. Moreover it is this inner world with its repeating repertory that determines most of what happens to us in the external world.
>
> Who writes the scripts? What are the plots about? And where are they performed?
>
> Language informs us that the scriptwriter is called I. Psychoanalysis has taught us that the scenarios were written years ago by a naive and childlike I struggling to survive in an adult world whose drama conventions are quite different from the child's. These psychic plays may be performed in the theater of our own minds or that of our bodies or may take place in the external world, sometimes using other peoples' minds and bodies, or even social institutions, as their stage.

Each self has a secret theater—rather like the magic theater in Herman Hesse's *Steppenwolf*—in which archaic assumptions, antique perspectives, clichéd emotions, like used furniture and leftover bric-a-brac, clutter the stage and, still connected to past roles, determine the actions of the present. Such theaters of the mind bring about the daily repetition of tragedies and comedies and romances played out many times before.

At this most general level, then, the fictive processes may be seen as an organizer of the scenarios that drive behavior. A person reading a book, listening to the radio, reading the newspaper, watching television or a movie, or seeing a play or opera rapidly scans the fictions that are presented, like a director auditioning various actors, until, suddenly, there occurs a coincidence between the inner scenario and the available fiction: something "clicks." Then the fiction is pulled into the self, as if it *were* the self, and a fictive personality moves across the internal stage. Perhaps, too, it will take on a public role in behavior that may be ideal—or awful.

McDougall's descriptions of the theaters of the mind can be seen in a more rounded and complex way when combined with the theory of fictions proposed by the philosopher Hans Vaihinger. Vaihinger's work is *The Philosophy of "As If."* "Fictions," as he uses the term, are conceptions that, though they may refer to nonexistent entities and are never verifiable, are necessary to mental functioning. William of Occam called them *ficta* and acknowledged their practical necessity; Hobbes spoke of "Conscious Fictions," such as "equality" or "original contract." But according to Vaihinger, it was Kant, followed by Nietzsche, who most profoundly understood the necessity for fictions in mental operations. Fictions, he argues, are valuable and indispensable, even as they allow for the dangerous likelihood—even the inevitability—that they will become confused with reality. In this analysis such concepts as "law," "freedom," "justice," and so on, are all fictions—constructs that are necessary to maintain social relations and achieve individual selfhood—even as they are acknowledged to be constructs or fictions. "The higher aspects of life are based upon noble delusions," Vaihinger writes. (This can be reversed, of course: the worst aspects of life can also be based on the noblest delusions.)

Following Nietzsche, Vaihinger sees "truth" as the most

expedient "fiction." He quotes Nietzsche's remark: "The erroneousness of a concept does not for me constitute an objection to it; the question is—to what extent is it advantageous to life? . . . Indeed, I am convinced that the most erroneous assumptions are precisely the most indispensable for us, that without . . . measuring reality by the invented world . . . man could not live."

Among contemporary analysts, Donald Spence has perhaps most fully seen how psychoanalytic interpretation itself must consider the context of a patient's "life story," so that discourse can have a "narrative home" in inner experience. "The linguistic and narrative aspects of an interpretation may well have priority over its historical truths," he writes. Spence is part of a philosophical, rhetorical, and psychological tradition that sees truth in the process of its creation.

As an earlier contributor to that tradition, Alfred Adler acknowledged his debt to Vaihinger's *The Philosophy of "As If"* in his own work. "It was good fortune which made me acquainted with Vaihinger's ingenious philosophy of 'as if,' " Adler wrote. He described it as "a work in which I heard the thoughts familiar to me from my [analysis of] neurosis presented as valid for scientific thinking in general." Adler posited fictions as expedient and necessary psychical constructs by means of which an individual's development achieves direction and purpose. Adler calls the aim of life, therefore, the "fictional goal," and argues that all people have such an inner goal. "The healthy individual as well as the neurotic," he wrote in *The Neurotic Character*, "would have to forego orientation in the world if he did not organize his picture of the world and his experiences according to fictions." Adler's entire concept of the will to power as a fundamental drive is thus suffused with fictive processes. We make value-ridden fictions of success, self-esteem, and social good; and in trying to bring these fictions into being, we achieve power. Adler's theory thus starts with the assumption that fictive processes function at the very highest level of human aspiration and activity.

In 1942 Helene Deutsch wrote a justly famous essay titled "Some Forms of Emotional Disturbance and Their Relation to Schizophrenia." In this work she described what she called the "as if personality." Though, in point of fact, she did not describe an "as if" personality so much as "as if" processes *in* the personality, the term has stuck; and though she did not really see the "as if personality" as necessarily schizophrenic, the association, based on her title, between "as if" and deep pathology has been assumed. She herself denied that by "as if" she meant the same as Vaihinger; but clearly she knew his work, and she did make implicit use of a theory of fictions similar to his.

Deutsch focuses upon "the individual's emotional relationship to the outside world" where "his own ego appears impoverished or absent," and where there is a paucity of "affective bonds and responses." This, as we have seen, is an integral feature of the fictive personality. Such an emotional disturbance, she says, takes two forms. In the first, the individual experiences an inner feeling of unreality. In the second, that feeling is projected defensively into the world, and existence "seems strange, objects shadowy, [and] human beings and events theatrical and unreal." What seems at first to be imaginative talent in such people, appears, under scrutiny, to be imaginative parasitism, mental automatism—the "borrowing," on the surface, of the talents or techniques of idealized others. Similarly, emotional relationships of "as if" people look intense and varied, but investigation shows them to be "devoid of any trace of warmth." "As if" persons seem to have vivid interior lives, but closer inspection shows that "inner experience" is excluded. "It is," Deutsch writes, "like the performance of an actor who is technically well trained but who lacks the necessary spark to make his impersonations true to life."

Deutsch is very clear about the dynamic source of the "as if" personality: though in appearance it looks like the sort of depersonalized coldness that results from the repression, say, of highly charged drives, "psychoanalysis discloses that in the 'as if' individual it is no longer an act of repression but a real loss of object cathexes" that is fundamental in shaping personality. Thus the individual relates to the world, as I would put it, by transient identifications. The self waits to be "filled up" by available object identifications, and any object appears as good as another, any aim is as desirable as the next one. This makes the fictive personality equally capable of apparent nobility or apparent perfidy. Like the objects that pass before Plato's cave, casting their shadows on the walls within, objects in the "as if" or fictive person's world provide the shadowy selves, the fictions, that seize, one after another, the empty inner world. "Overenthusiastic adherence to one philosophy"—or partner, or moral system— "can be quickly and completely replaced by another contradictory one without the slightest trace of inward transformation—simply as a result of some accidental regrouping of the circle of acquaintances, or the like."

Despite the title of her work and its main thrust, Deutsch does not argue, ultimately, that the "as if" personality is confined to schizophrenia; rather, it can become manifested in a variety of ways. Yet every part of the range exhibits some "schizoid" characteristics, that is, the occurrence of fictive personality is almost invariably connected with some evidence of emptiness or disconnectedness in the person.

The clearest work on schizoid characteristics has been done by the psychoanalyst Harry Guntrip in his 1968 book *Schizoid Phenomena, Object Relations and The Self*. Guntrip's central theme is that the schizoid person is caught in a fundamental conflict: at one and the same time he has renounced all connections with the world and also hungers for association with it. He feels empty and yearns to be filled, but he insists on staying distant from anything that could give him substantial meaning. How does this come about? In normal development, Guntrip argues, the self strives to establish connections with other people, to make commitments to ideas and beliefs, and to form meaningful relations with many institutions. Such relatedness is based on the first connections that the child has with parents and family. When the value of associations with others is confirmed by the pleasurable experience of the child, then the development of good relations has every reason to continue.

On the other hand, early relations do not always go smoothly. Sometimes associations with others bring physical, mental, or emotional injuries, and the experience of hurt, repeated with sufficient frequency, can drive the child away from associations, locking the self inside itself. Instead of growing in relatedness, the self is stunted by its retreat inside. Now the outside and inside worlds both look simultaneously inviting and frightening. The outer and inner worlds are both distorted and seen as hollow, desirable but frightening, impossible. No wonder the schizoid seems paralyzed.

Thus, the ground is laid for the development of a personality that strives to hide from others even as it yearns to associate with them. It is easy to see how, in this context, identifications with fiction can provide an apparent solution for the schizoid orientation. By assuming a mask, a role, a make-believe identity, the schizoid can seem to participate in the world even as he or she hides from it. Identifying with fictions, the schizoid seeks an authentic self, but instead develops a role; looks for real intimacy, but achieves pseudo-relations; appears involved, but remains distant. Yet, one thing is achieved: the self is protected, even if it does not otherwise satisfy its yearnings. One of my analysands said to me: "I feel that my symptoms are just a scenario." Everything was play-acting to him—his wishes and his fears, even his behavior seemed based upon someone else's script—but who was writing the script he did not know.

Guntrip's descriptions have the ring of truth. The schizoid, he writes, "usually has a rich and active fantasy life, but in real life is often tepid and weak in enthusiasm, is apt to suffer inexplicable losses of interest, and feels little zest in living. Yet deep inside he has particularly intense needs. He can live in imagination but not in the world of material reality from which he is primarily withdrawn into himself. He wants to realize his dreams in real life, but if he finds a dream coming true externally he seems to be unaccountably unable to accept and enjoy it, especially if it concerns a personal relationship." Schizoid fantasy is devoted to maintaining the distance between the self and the outer world, and play-acting offers roles by which the schizoid can come to life in part—through a part.

R. D. Laing's 1959 book, *The Divided Self*, is related to the concepts of both Deutsch and Guntrip, as well as to D. W. Winnicott's "false self." Laing sees the false self as equivalent to the schizoid personality. Already implicit in Winnicott's essay was the idea that through delusions fused into identifications, the self can develop a false-self system of ideas, beliefs, and emotions, created, as Freud had said in 1911, in an attempt at a rebuilding of the sick person's vanished object world. Laing paid close clinical attention to the development of false-self systems as a person's means of at least maintaining the illusion of being tied to reality. His descriptions of the operations of false-self systems illuminates our subject from yet another perspective.

Laing teases out three characteristics of the false self. While normal persons may carry out habitual actions in false selves, habitual actions seem to assume an "autonomous, compulsive" existence, "such that the individual feels that [his actions] are 'living' or rather killing him, rather than he living them." Actions seem artificial, mechanically determined from without.

After Bruno Kreisky's contact with terrorism during the OPEC kidnappings, he commented: "There is a very deep . . . partly a very artificial brutality about these people. They've made up their minds to accept this brutality. It's part of a system and this makes it so terrible." Here, Kreisky was confirming Laing's first characteristic form of the false self—its artificiality, its mechanical nature, the sense that it is not part of the personality, but a mechanical instrument that functions in (not of) the person.

Laing also says that the false-self system casually detaches the person from what he says or does. As a consequence, his actions do not give him or her pleasure, in contrast to the hysteric, who derives pleasure from the way he shocks other people by his actions. The hysteric can be at least temporarily satisfied by the way he affects and perhaps manipulates others. The false self, on the other hand, still hungers for response no matter what responses he receives.

Finally, the false self has no basic desires to fulfill, and therefore cannot experience fulfillment. No authentic self is experienced.

Laing describes a "false self" in the case of an adolescent, David. David had always been an obedient child, and he was especially devoted to his mother until she died. Then he took her place, doing the housework; he even did embroidery. David behaved in a highly artificial way. "For instance, he attended lectures in a cloak, which he wore over his shoulders and arms; he carried a cane . . . his speech was made up largely of quotations." To Laing he looked like a strange hodgepodge of identities—"an adolescent Kierkegaard played by Danny Kaye. He was not simply eccentric: I could not escape the impression that this young man was playing at being eccentric." Experiencing himself—even his gender identity, it seems—as fictive, he set about doing what is natural for a fiction: taking up roles, without any need to arrive at an identity. In treatment he explained that even before his mother died, he had been playing roles. First, he was simply whatever his mother wanted him to be. Later, he played at taking her role. His view of reality was simply that everyone else was just like himself; everyone played parts. "Usually, in his mind, he was playing the part of someone else, but sometimes he played at being himself. His ideal was *never to give himself away to others*," and so his actions were all impersonations.

Clearly, David's behavior was a defense against his own possible discovery that he had no real self; or to ward off the probable discovery by others that he had nothing of value to offer. The false-self system thus arises as a defense against the fear that without someone else's life to live, there will be no stable system anywhere, internally or externally.

The defensive functions of fictive personality, then, are very important; these can be considered from a number of angles. One function was effectively designated by Anna Freud as "altruistic surrender" in the tenth chapter of *The Ego and the Mechanisms of Defense*. She shows that gratification is achieved, not directly, but through projection of one's own wishes onto another, followed by identification with the gratification which that other person experiences. As an example, Anna Freud describes a young governess who, as a child, had wished fervently for beautiful clothes and many children. Though as an adult she wore modest dress and remained unmarried and childless, she fulfilled her original desires by taking an active interest in the clothes of her friends, being an insatiable matchmaker, and caring for many children in her profession. "It looked," Anna Freud writes, "as if her own life had been emptied of interests and wishes. . . . Instead of exerting herself to achieve any aims of her own, she expended all her energy in sympathizing with the experiences of people she cared for. She lived in the lives of other people, instead of having any experience of her own." "Altruistic surrender" most usually involves relatively inconspicuous, "normal" forms of projection and identification. However, it is just as easy to "live through" murderous causes as through happy ones, as easy to assist terrorists and lay down one's life for them as to be a busy matchmaker for others' happy marriages.

Anna Freud is only one of several analysts who have described the defensive functions of fictive personality formations. The great psychoanalyst and critic Ernst Kris is another. Both defensive and also expressive of a life pattern is a syndrome described by Kris in 1956, in what he called the "personal myth." He suggests that some patients fashion a myth—a secret, hidden life—out of their own autobiographical memories as these are shaped by early, unconscious fantasies. Their memories, that is, are reorganized by self-fictions rather than by experience and actuality and form a "protective screen." Its apparently "firm outline and richness of detail are meant to cover significant omissions and distortions." Such a myth is organized early, at a time when fantasy and reality are not sharply divided, then itself becomes an organizer of later experiences. Kris cites the case of a man who saw himself as a superman, "clearly recognizable as the idealized image of the father, whose role he has adopted in elevated stature." Kris helps to point us to the fact that fictive personalities draw on what they can get: novels, plays, media—and even life, when necessary.

The fictive personality process is certainly related to the narcissistic disorders, which Heinz Kohut described in several books and articles. As he analyzes narcissism, Kohut shows that the narcissist is at heart unsure of himself even as he wants to convince others of his supreme value. Kohut argues that narcissism is a developmental disorder. Because development was stunted and fixed, the self cannot go forward on all fronts. The deficiency of self is dealt with through a considerable array of unconscious defenses that strive to hold the self together internally and externally, in order to achieve the semblance of integrity and to gain love. However, the defenses are likely to be fairly rigid and to rely upon appearance. It is no wonder that a common feature of narcissism involves the trying on of attractive roles. The role helps the narcissist to call attention to himself even while protecting himself. If the role is attractive or compelling enough to elicit the attention that he wants, and to persuade others to accept the grandiose appearance for the true self, the narcissist is satisfied to be accepted at "face value." If the role proves to be unacceptable or unattractive to others, the narcissist can always drop the role and seek out another—and another—that will bring the admiration he craves. The self of the narcissist lacks the sort of cohesion that demands one to be "true to himself." The narcissist will choose behavior—in some instances, fictive personality behavior—that expresses the wish that others will give the sort of love that inwardly he cannot give to himself.

Kohut postulates that the two components of narcissism—troubled love towards oneself, along with defective love towards others—develop along separate lines. This seems compatible with my suggestion that fictive personality arises when there is a simultaneous disturbance of both normal narcissism and relations to others. Narcissistic personalities channel themselves into the vehicle of fictions in order to armor the self and also to develop an array of identifications connecting the self to the world: but both are conceived of as fictive. The narcissist knows that his behavior is a guise, a masquerade, designed for others. It is easy for him to believe that all people do the same thing, and therefore he sees the world as a phony drama.

Kohut's work, along with that of his followers, then, contributes a very useful perspective to the understanding of fictive personality as a defensive maneuver. Identification with a fiction allows the narcissistically injured person to "exist," even if at the cost of obliging the personality to disappear. Whatever reality the actual personality is encountering—fragmentation, regression, the upsurge of violent impulses—that reality can be disavowed and split off, while the fiction is inserted in its place in the way that witches or gypsies are supposed to leave a human-like doll in the cradle when they steal a real baby away. The situation roughly resembles that process which also occurs in multiple personality, except that in the case of multiple personality sudden and severe trauma usually causes the old injured self to split off and go into repression, while a fresh new identity is internally invented (instead of being imported from outside the self, as in fictive personality) for the purpose of administering the self.

The defense of disavowal operates powerfully here. When the wishes and needs of the real self become so intensely painful that the self has to protect itself through disavowal, then the person becomes blind to the significance of even his own behavior. Disavowal is the defense that operates most powerfully in narcissistic patients. Long before Kohut, Freud explained the basic operations of disavowal in his 1927 essay "Fetishism." Disavowal, he said, manages to avoid a threatening reality not through repression or by denying the threatening reality itself, but by creating two streams in mental life, thus separating any threat to the self from the rest of the self, and so giving the impression of *la belle indifference*. When narcissism is allied with the fictive personality process, disavowal is managed with particular ease: the grandiose, split-off part of the self allies with the fiction, and the threatened self is kept at bay. By this means it is easy and natural for a person like John Hinckley to say that the only politician he admires is Ronald Reagan, or to claim that "he" (John Hinckley) collected guns because Travis

Bickle did, while the "other" Hinckley favors gun control. Disavowal—*verleugnung* is Freud's word—means, as he used it, self-deception in the face of accurate perception. Terry, the patient described earlier, perceived his weakness, but also saw himself as a superman. As the most insightful of analysts of disavowal, Michael Franz Basch, puts it: "A split in the ego permits the patient to deal with external reality . . . while [simultaneously] permitting his wish-fulfilling fantasy to exist side by side with reality, protecting him from the anxiety that would otherwise be generated."

In addition to his significant work about narcissistic defenses, Kohut has made important contributions to the discussion of the developmental issues connected with problems in mirroring and relations to other people. Kohut has well exhibited that for a self's proper development and maintenance, good mirroring—seeing one's self confirmed in and valued by others—must occur. Again, Kohut is, of course, scarcely the only analyst to make this point. "The conscious feeling of having a personal identity," Erik Erikson wrote in "Ego Development and Historical Change," is based on "two simultaneous observations: the immediate perception of one's selfsameness and continuity in time; and the simultaneous perception of the fact that others recognize one's sameness and continuity." After all, even Descartes' "I am" cannot be taken for granted. It has to be created both internally and externally.

The formation of a self is the child's first major creative effort. Fictive personality is clearly a substitute formation, in which characters from fiction or mass-media, instead of living persons, become the mirror that reflects identity. "The Jackal" was Carlos's mirror; the Lone Ranger, Terry's; Travis Bickle, Hinckley's; and so on. Fictive mirrors offer grandiose, highly unrealistic images in which the self can "see" (and often "mis-see") itself. A fictive mirror almost always results from the fear that without a sublime mirror, the person will disappear, have no reflection at all. There is the strong suggestion that this is a "last resort" strategy when no real mirrors are available. But once a fiction has been introjected as a mirror and it becomes a part of the self, it is hard to root it out. The Queen in "Snow White" has no one to confirm her grandiose yearnings for beauty, and so, in an empty ritualistic way, she constantly asks her own mirror for confirmation.

Kohut uses the term "selfobject" to refer to persons (or even things) that one experiences as incompletely separated from the self. Quite naturally, a mother is a selfobject for an infant. Many children later experience a normal version of the fictive selfobject in the fantasy of what Freud called "the family romance." This is a child's fantasy that he or she is really of aristocratic or elevated birth and for one reason or another is being raised by other, lowly parents. This fairy-tale of family romance is part of the normal development of self-regard and of separation from parents. Another fantasy with a similar function is that of the imaginary twin where the "twin" is a projection of one's need to have a mirror for one's self. The fantasy of the double is still another familiar fantasy. But fictions of identity can take much more extreme forms when the self does not feel truly reflected. The French psychoanalyst André Green has compared the narcissistically ill to the vampire, who can never see a reflection in the mirror. The fictive personality can also feel like a *mort-vivant*, one of the living dead: for such a person, fictions are used to find reflections. In extreme instances, the self has undoubtedly experienced some kind of traumatic death at an earlier period. It is better, after all, to be a fiction than to be nothing. When driven to the extremity of this choice, the self will use fictions to maintain a tie to "otherness." When "reality" itself is no longer available, fictions can become the last resort of reality and the last defense against annihilation.

For the normal person, of course, relations to others, along with one's own ideals, should be and will be the fundamental, rock-bottom sources of reality. When fictions replace love for others and love of values, then reality can be turned topsy turvy. This helps to show why fictive personality is so closely related to perversions.

Perversion turns the world inside out, especially through investing some magical object—the "fetish"—with power that it does not possess on its own. In the sexual perversions, to take a familiar example, "foot fetishism" involves the use of the foot as an object of sexual pleasure. Substituting the foot for the penis distorts or "perverts" genital primacy in sex through substituting a magical object for the normal one.

More generally, outside the realm of sexuality strictly considered, fictive personality processes are indeed perversions of the normal world. The fetish is the theatrical role and its sources. Don Quixote's volumes of romance, for instance, are magical objects. For Mark David Chapman, Lennon and Holden Caulfield were fetishes. For the terrorist, the gun is a fetish. In all these cases, the overvalued fetish turns the values and order of the world inside out. For instance, the terrorist killer is really noble, while the forces of morality or legality are debased pigs; a squalid world is an ideal one; a Chapman would do the world a favor by killing a Lennon. A murderer becomes God. When the role from fiction is invested with omnipotent magical powers thought able to cure all problems and solve all questions, then the world is completely distorted. The function of such fetishizing is clear: when the world's values are overthrown, the pathologies of the self can be installed in their place.

Consider, as a good example of perversion, the communiqués of the Symbionese Liberation Army, the group that kidnapped Patty Hearst. The following communiqué was tape-recorded by William Harris after the deaths of several members of the SLA. Harris, Hearst writes, was "certain that he was right and the rest of the world wrong."

> Cin was the baddest member of the SLA and therefore our leader. . . . Cujo, Gelina, Fahizah, Zoya, and Gabi did not commit suicide, as the pigs would have us believe. Pigs tell us it is suicidal for Whites to join Blacks and other oppressed people in making revolution. . . .
>
> The pigs boast that they have broken the back of the Symbionese Liberation Army. But to do this, the pigs would have to break the back of the people. The military political leader of the SLA and five top cadre have been killed by the fascists. However, the SLA is not dead and will not die as long as there is one living, fighting member of any oppressed class, race, sex, or group left on the face of this earth. The pigs have won a battle, but the war of the flea is not over.

On the same occasion, Hearst herself said in her recorded message:

> Greetings to the people. This is Tania. I want to talk about the way I knew our six murdered comrades. . . .
>
> Cujo was the gentlest, most beautiful man I've ever known. He taught me the truth as he learned it from the beautiful brothers in California's concentration camps. We love each other so much, and his love for the people was so deep that he was willing to give his life for them. The name Cujo means "unconquerable." It was the perfect name for him. Cujo conquered life as well as death by facing and fighting them. Neither Cujo or I had ever loved an individual the way we loved each other, probably because our relationship wasn't based on bourgeois, fucked-up values, attitudes, and goals. . . .
>
> I was ripped off by the pigs when they murdered Cujo, ripped off in the same way that thousands of sisters and brothers in this fascist country have been ripped off of people they love. We mourn together and the sound of gunfire becomes sweeter.

All values in civilization are reversed, along with any reasonable assessment of actual social relations in the world, by the fetishizing of the SLA and the dead—now magical—corpses of its members. The SLA movement as a whole, it should be remembered, was thoroughly fetishized—in its salutes, its rhetoric, its pretentious titles, its symbols, its style of recorded announcements, its new names, and so on.

The most interesting of the recent studies of perversion is Janine Chasseguet-Smirgel's book *Creativity and Perversion*. She argues that the underlying aim of perversion is the destruction of all ordinary values in the pervert's attempt to "free himself from the paternal universe and the constraints of the law." To illustrate her thesis she offers three examples of what she calls the perverse or "Luciferian" character.

The first is a historical personage, the Roman emperor Caligula. Virtually the whole of Caligula's reign was marked by his drive to modify reality in order to glorify himself. He truly felt himself to be a god, and he set about redoing the world in order to make it conform to his wishes—but more important, to alter it from the world as originally created. Caligula installed animals as counselors or senators, replaced ordinary heterosexual activity with incest, and built elaborate artificial constructions that replaced nature. He made murder the "life" of his reign.

Her second and third examples are both from the arts. She points to *The Island of Doctor Moreau* by H. G. Wells as a paradigm of perversion. In his perverse experiments, Dr. Moreau created a race of "men" who were also animals—a man-pig, a man-bull, and so on. They felt themselves to be humans, but also knew themselves to be animals and felt the influence of their second natures. For them, Dr. Moreau was their creator, a Luciferian god whom they loved, feared, and hated for giving them divided natures.

In the surrealist artist Hans Bellmer she finds her third example. Bellmer's drawings are elaborate reorderings of the world. He is, of course, working in the traditions of surrealism, and his productions do not have the social effects of the activities of Caligula or Doctor Moreau. But Bellmer himself wrote a number of theoretical papers on his attempt to create a perverse psychology in his audience, and to undermine the ordinary view of reality with one in which certain objects—most especially phallic and genital ones—are valued, while the rest of the world is degraded. Eventually, then, his aim can be seen to be identical with Caligula's and Moreau's—to replace the world and to have, instead, a Luciferian world, a world that in every respect opposes nature and natural acts.

Individual perversion is likely to arise from distortions in mirroring, by parents who present the child with opportunities to identify with perverse activity. A parent who abuses a child physically or emotionally teaches the child that pain is the vehicle of love. A parent who undermines the normal development of the child's sexuality may reverse the direction of genital development, teaching the child to experience the natural genital as if it were unnatural. In such a case, the actual genital becomes an object of hatred and its mask, the costume, becomes fetishized. R. D. Laing's case of David, already referred to, included several aspects of the perverse:

> All through his childhood he had been very fond of playing parts in front of the mirror. Now in front of the mirror he continued to play parts. The parts he played in front of the mirror were always women's parts. He dressed himself up in his mother's clothes, which had been kept. He rehearsed female parts from the great tragedies. But then he found he could not stop playing the part of a woman. He caught himself compulsively walking like a woman, talking like a woman, even seeing and thinking as a woman might see and think. This was his present position, and this was his explanation for his fantastic get-up. For, he said, he found that he was driven to dress up and act in his present manner as the only way to arrest the womanish part that threatened to engulf not only his actions

but even his own self as well, and to rob him of his much cherished control and mastery of his being. Why he was driven into playing this role, which he hated and which he knew everyone laughed at, he could not understand. But this role was the only refuge he knew from being entirely engulfed by the woman who was inside him, and always seemed to be coming out of him.

David was caught tragically in a deflection of normal development. His Caligula, his god, was his mother; to get her love, he imagined that he had to be just like her—even to the extent of becoming a woman. He had to be recreated, *contra naturum*. The only way he could become so was through costumes. He loved and hated the parts he had to play—but he was compelled to play them. His role, his sexuality, his costumes were the fetishes of his reconstruction. His perversity bloomed into his fantasies, and his fantasies into his fictions.

The work of Alfred Adler, Helene Deutsch, Harry Guntrip, R. D. Laing, Anna Freud, Heinz Kohut, and Chasseguet-Smirgel, when taken together, provide the major outlines by which fictive personality may be understood. Each of these analysts, of course, followed a different interest, and each had a variety of interests that go beyond my subject. But when we put these studies together, it is possible to see that they all point in the same direction. The basic dynamic-defensive aspects of the fictive personality localize it in the area of the narcissistic disorders. The analysts I have looked at have described, each from a separate angle, a part of what is, when taken together, itself a significant component of narcissism.

Narcissism, we should remember, has two sides. Narcissus is not remembered in Greek mythology only for his self-destructive self-absorption. He is also remarkable for his beauty. Each of the analysts whom I refer to above also had to try to take into consideration the relation between the pathological and creative aspects of his or her subject. After all, while the "as if" personality, for instance, can lead to schizophrenia, the "as if" suspension of disbelief is fundamental to the world's greatest stories and a central facet of the human imagination. "Let's pretend that . . . there was a young man named Hamlet. . . . that man can fly . . . that the human heart can be replaced with an artificial organ . . . that man can make a covenant with God . . . that man can make a perfect democracy . . ."—these are all *as if* propositions, and central to the highest achievements of humans. Altruism, the subject of Anna Freud's analysis, can lead to an impoverishment of life—but it can also form an aim, such as Mother Teresa's or Albert Schweitzer's, that ennobles both the altruist and his or her objects. The personal myth can be destructive—as it certainly was in the cases of Hitler and Stalin—but it can also provide the backbone for the noblest of endeavors. Perversion can infuse madness into society, but the perverse wish to recreate reality is an aspect of all artistic and inventive endeavors. An artificial heart is not a fetish—but by definition it is certainly not natural; yet it is indubitably life-producing. Narcissism, too, is a valuable possession, leading to confidence, productive optimism and self-esteem, and the capacity for commitment. So there is a very close connection between fictive personality and the capacity for inventiveness, originality, and creativity.

Creative writers, as we have seen, first described the fictive personality, and therefore it should not be at all surprising that the psychoanalysts who have contributed most to the understanding of the fictive personality should all have turned to discussions of literary works. In a 1937 essay devoted to "Don Quixote and Don Quixotisms," Helene Deutsch treats the hero of the novel clinically in terms similar to those she uses in her discussion of the "as if" personality. Later, in her 1956 essay on the imposter, she cites Thomas Mann's novel *The Confessions of Felix Krull* as providing an apt illustration of her clinical points. In his book, Guntrip devotes a long central section to a discussion of Henry James's life and works as good examples of the operations of the schizoid personality. R. D. Laing's work is crowded with references to literature. Francis Bacon, Samuel Beckett, Dante, Gorky, Hölderlin, Keats, Kierkegaard, Marianne Moore, Rimbaud, Sartre, Shakespeare, W. B. Yeats, and, most of all, Franz Kafka, are referred to in *The Divided Self* alone.

Anna Freud, too, found the chief confirmation of her theory of altruistic surrender in a work of literature. She remarks that in her view "the finest and most detailed study of . . . altruistic surrender is to be found in Edmond Rostand's play *Cyrano de Bergerac.*" The hero, Cyrano, helps his friend— and rival—Christian to woo Roxanne, the woman they both love, since Cyrano, due to his huge nose, feels himself unworthy of being loved. Cyrano exemplifies the fictive personality; in conversation, he "speaks" poetry, even in rhyme: he composes as he duels, turning aggression into fiction. He believes that contemporary writers such as Corneille, Molière, and Swift have borrowed their work from him. He lives in a completely fictional world and there—far removed from real love for another person—he seeks his satisfaction. Isolated from love, nevertheless he desires it; still, he flees from the opportunity to possess it.

Ernst Kris began his intellectual career as an art historian and wrote a book, *Psychoanalytic Explorations of Art*, in which he brilliantly studied art against a background of psychoanalytic theory, and vice-versa. Kohut's first psychoanalytic paper, published in 1957, concerned Thomas Mann's *Death in Venice*; in this article Kohut studied the disintegration of artistic sublimation—that is to say, the destruction of Aschenbach's ability to *create* literary fictions, leading him to experience and *treat himself* as a fiction. Chasseguet-Smirgel, finally, illustrates her conception of perversion through literature and art as often as through clinical observation. Not only

H. G. Wells, Bellmer, and de Sade, but also Camus, Ionesco, Molière, and Oscar Wilde are discussed in *Creativity and Perversion*.

Each of these analysts defined pathological aspects of fictive personality processes; but each also pointed to the creative aspects of the use of good fictions. We are obliged to conclude that an infant or child who is badly disillusioned can experience herself or himself as fictive, and this can lead to various degrees of pathology. Contrariwise, a child who is disillusioned can "bounce back," be reillusioned and allowed to believe in good fictions again through good relations with loved ones and the appropriate satisfaction of fantasies. This process constitutes an early creative experience in dealing with the double character of fictions, "good" and "bad." Many writers, artists, innovators, or inventors seem to have had an early experience with the pain of disillusionment, followed by the pleasure of reillusionment. Their biographers suggest that this was so for Mann, James, Kafka, Bellmer, Rostand, and others. But it is not the authors, but their characters—Don Quixote, Krull, Strether, Cyrano, and Aschenbach—who are the fictive personalities. How did these authors manage to achieve a capacity to manipulate illusions instead of being driven by them? How did they manage to pass from the feelings of surrender to another's fiction and from bondage to illusions to the capacity to free the imagination by creating their own illusions?

I would assume that as infants, Cervantes, Rostand, and the others had some satisfying, rather than merely terrorizing, experience with illusions; for each spent considerable time reliving that past pleasure through creating illusions in the present. At the same time, in creating their characters for themselves and for others, these writers preserved a memory of a disturbance in infancy, memorializing a trauma that they suffered and overcame—but never, in the unconscious, forgot.

In anyone's life the process of illusioning, disillusioning, and reillusioning is fundamental to a world outlook. How one negotiates this complex process of illusions will influence, and perhaps determine, one's eventual perception of both reality and fictions, as well as the relations between them. This outlook is the consequence of how an individual develops. And so, to go further, we have to go back—to explore the development of the self in relation to the world.

# 8

# Telling Lives

We all make use of fictions. Our first fictions are fantasies about our parents, our body, the self, other humans in the environment, and finally, strangers. Our parents probably involve us in our second set of fictions, our guesses about how they feel about us. Later in life, we are offered fictions created by others we don't even know, concerning beings we will never see. These are the fictions of fairy tales and legends, followed by those in books, films, and other entertainments. All of these fictions leave a particular mark, for every person will come to possess his or her own constellation of fictions with their special meaning. Each individual gathering of fictions or fantasies offers opportunities for identification, imitation, or counteractivity. Seen in this light, fictions are an essential element in the process of growth and change. They are fundamental to maturation, since they provide a necessary arena for "trying on" identities and "trying out" relations to others.

Yet, at every stage of development, experience with fictions is ambiguous. Not all fictions serve development; obviously, some fictions are "good," while others are "bad." "Good fictions" are variously named: "play," "experiment," "improvisation," "imagination," "hypothetical thinking," and "creativity." "Self-deception," "delusional thinking," "impairment of reality testing," and "illusions" are the terms by which we characterize fictions that hinder or stunt growth and development. "Good fictions" are called "healthy" and "adaptive" because they tend to prepare us for action, compensate for loss, or make flexibility and inventiveness possible. "Bad fictions" are termed "neurotic" or even "psychotic" because they lead to isolation, denial, or grandiosity; they make loss inevitable and block spontaneous experimentation.

The division into "good" and "bad" fictions in adult life starts out as a single process in infancy. The infant's experience of internal illusions is soon subjected to a steady stream of disillusionment, from within and without. Put in the simplest terms, the infant is "illusioned" by his internal push for pleasure. His "illusions" seem confirmed by the experience of gratification and realized in the internal feeling of cohesion and growth. What "disillusions" the infant is the failure of the environment to respond to his illusions, which the infant can interpret only as loss. Loss attacks growth, blocks pleasure, brings pain. Loss binds and confines. Loss is what the process of disillusionment brings and how it comes to be defined.

Necessarily, infancy *must* include both illusioning and disillusioning experiences—confirmations that the self coheres in itself and can adhere to others, and also experiences that involve loss, the inception of doubt and, in Goethe's phrase, "disorder and early sorrow." Illusionment and disillusionment are so mixed and balanced in healthy development that they seem one process. Through apparent confirmation of internal illusions or fantasies, the self begins the process of self-acceptance and then of attunement to and negotiation with the outer world. From small but steady experience of disillusionment comes a grudging acceptance of the claims of the outside world, along with the formation of adaptive mechanisms for facing change, active talents for making change, and capacities for coping with disappointment.

Infants "recover" quite naturally from their inevitable disillusionment when it occurs in a phase-appropriate manner. Indeed, later adult pleasure in suspending disbelief in images, illusions, and fictions of all sorts is probably a recollection of the pleasure once derived from recovering from disillusionment through learning to believe and then not believe in fictions. For some people, this pleasure in manipulating fictions was so great in infancy and childhood that they later devote their lives to experiment, and they become creators—writers, painters, scientists, inventors, filmmakers. Others are content simply to believe or to suspend disbelief without being disappointed or overwhelmingly disillusioned. Those who have recovered will learn to see fictions as predominantly "good."

That, of course, is the optimum path of development—when illusionment and disillusionment flow together in a mutually facilitating manner. But what happens when the infant's involvement with fictions is not facilitating? When the infant is too suddenly, or too continuously disillusioned, loss, anxiety, and depression seize hold of the growing self. In this state of disillusionment, the infant—and then the child and later the adult—can neither risk belief nor tolerate disbelief. Instead of belief, loss is embedded or "inscribed" within the developing personality. Ultimately this means the self cannot believe in itself, and instead sees itself as an illusion.

Instead of creating fictions, the person just described seeks

ready-made fictions wherein to find identities. Instead of
the creative pleasure of manipulating fictions from inside,
he or she seeks to adopt the illusions of others. This process
starts in infancy and, when it becomes pathological, it forever
after forces the return to infantile feelings in a hapless and
hopeless effort to regain the primary state of infant illusion,
before disillusion spoiled the paradise of that world.

Let us take a closer look at the distinction between the
infant who can manage illusions and the infant who seeks
illusions to maintain him. It is vividly presented in the freely
experimenting play of some children and the empty, tentative
behavior of children who are playing the games of others.

In a recent book, *The Interpersonal World of the Infant*, the
child psychiatrist and researcher Daniel N. Stern explores
the infant's subjective experience, and especially focuses upon
what he calls the problems of "affect attunement." Attunement, as he sees it, is a process that develops between a
mother and her infant, when the mother responds, through
her own experience, to the infant's inner emotional needs
as if they are hers. But, Stern shows, perfect attunement
is impossible. Instead, there is "selective" attunement, which
inevitably leaves some parts of the infant's experience unre-
sponded to. These, then, "seem" to the infant to be illegitimate
parts, and form the basis for a later false self. Or, as I would
put it, these parts seek, first, fantasies, and later, fictions
for the completion of affect attunement.

"Misattunements" also occur between mother and infant,
and shape the infant's belief that his self is illegitimate. This
occurs when there is not a "good match" between mother
and child. Stern cites a clinical instance of a ten-month-old
boy. His mother, Stern says, undermatched his affective
behavior. When Sam looked to her excitedly, for example,
she responded only with a simple, solid, "Yes, honey." She
herself was an animated personality—but with Sam she flat-
tened her usual behavior. Queried about whether she had

intended to match the infant's level of enthusiasm in her response to him, she said "no." Tentatively she explained that "if she were to match him"—not even overmatch, but just match him—he would tend to focus more on her behavior than on his own. It might shift the initiative over from him to her. "She felt that he tended to lose his initiative if she joined in fully and equally and shared with him."

What, Stern asked, was wrong with the child's being less initiatory then she at this life phase? Then it became clear. She said she thought he resembled his father too much: he was too passive, too low-keyed. She wanted her son to be more like herself—a "spark-plug." She did not want her son to grow up to be like his father. So, purposely as well as unconsciously, she tried to make Sam more independent.

"One of the fascinating paradoxes about her strategy," Stern writes, "is that left alone, [her behavior] would do exactly the opposite of what she intended. Her underattunements would tend to create a lower-keyed child who was less inclined to share his spunk. The mother would inadvertently have contributed to making the son more like the father, rather than different from him." The mother, in this case, deliberately misattuned and thereby manipulated her child. She was unauthentic in herself, and she was seen in the process of making her infant a false child. She "underattuned." The opposite would be "overattunement" in which the mother "steals" the child's self by taking behavior away from him, for instance, overanticipating what the baby wants, and doing it first. The mother is the first person who appears over the horizon in the child's interpersonal world, and her actions powerfully affect the child's interpretations of the world and creativity in it.

An examination of attunements leads me into consideration of the part played in identity formation by "transitional phenomena," those elements in our lives that connect us first to our mothers and, later, more generally to our past experiences. I shall also have to say something more about the necessity of illusions. Then we can consider the origins of fictions and their later vicissitudes.

The basic questions in the development of personality revolve around the issue of boundaries. The crucial questions are: What is the me? Later, where does the me stop? Still later, what is not-me? Next: how do I relate to others? and how am I different? Finally, how do I achieve intimacy and sharing while still maintaining a sense of self? Such questions involve a concept of self *and* others, of inside *and* outside, of separation *and* individuation. Developmentally, deficits are as easily organized as capacities.

At the outset of life, the attention of the baby is directed toward itself, its own needs, its pleasures, drives, and instincts. This is normal narcissism. Later, the growing infant becomes aware of the existence of others and so starts to shift some of its attention—and attachment—to others. This process of attunement and attachment continues throughout development, in which attachments to self and others are balanced now this way, now that. But not all lives proceed with the ebb and flow of tides. The infant self seems to experience, very naturally, crucial points of organization or "transformation." These occur at two months, at twelve to thirteen months, and at eighteen to twenty-one months; at these times, in different ways, the infant hovers between the claims of narcissism and love of others, attachment and intimacy, the inner and the outer world.

I am thinking centrally of the times that Winnicott has described as filled with "transitional phenomena," when the infant seeks identification with what Anna Freud calls "something which is neither the body nor the outer world," but that helps in making the transition between the two. Transitional objects "fill in" for the mother when she is absent. A child may carry around and dearly love a blanket that the mother once used during feeding. A doll may be important if it was associated with mothering; a Raggedy Ann may be carried about until it falls into shreds. The blanket and the doll are transitional objects. Yet even as they are "objects," they are also illusions. They "stand for" the mother when she is absent. They comfort by giving the child an illusion that he or she can control the mother, or at least control a blanket associated with her and her love.

Transitional objects, then, accompany the child on the path of separation. Efforts at separation are fraught with anxiety. At times of special, transformative leaps of development, the world gets shaky. At such times, in the infant's mind, both the mother *and* the self are images, neither has substantial reality as a separate entity. To believe in the true reality of either would overly stress its separateness, and separateness is charged with anxiety that the self may disintegrate at the very time when it is reorganizing. At this stage the self is highly subject to distortion, since neither the self nor other people seem "solid."

Margaret Mahler, in her important work *The Psychological Birth of the Human Infant,* remarks that the way children are often introduced to fictions, especially during the second year, literally puts an extra stress upon storybooks as transitional phenomena. "The reading of storybooks became another transitional activity of particular importance: many toddlers liked to be read to while mother was out of the room. Storybooks would seem to be of a transitional nature, since they satisfied the need for distancing and for exploring the wider world (by way of symbolization and fantasy); on the other hand, the situation served the purpose of closeness, of getting near the person who was reading."

Anna Freud's Hampstead nursery provided some moving examples of disruptions at this stage, most centering around the way young children, deprived of their mothers, cling to clothing brought from home. When one of the children was told that "his mother would not come next Sunday, he began to cry, rushed to the drawer where the caps are kept, and called out: 'My Mummy does not come, me must wear a hat.' "

As they develop, of course, children must dispense with transitional phenomena and form new relationships. But what if no such relationship is available? What if it is not so easy to dispense with transitional objects or to leave transitional phenomena behind? No child is going to continue to wear a hat all his life. But other, less concrete substitutes for the twinned image of mother and of self are soon at hand from books, theater, and mass-culture, to help retrieve the lost illusions. Children who experience losses at transitional or transformative stages exhibit a much greater reliance on comforting fantasies—usually omnipotent ones—that restore a sense of capability or power. Such children also show a much greater evidence of fictive personality processes.

One stage builds upon another. A good experience of what the English psychoanalyst Esther Bick calls "adhesive identification" is important at the outset of life. The infant has to feel that it can "stick" to mother, that their skins mold together, that they can be so close it is impossible to tell where the infant's skin envelope begins and the mother's skin starts: they are so close, their skin seems one. This feeling is at the origin of basic trust. Such a feeling is likely to lead to a capacity to receive the comforts, while minimizing the terrors, of symbiosis, the stage where mother and infant are bonded together without the infant's feeling "smothered." This feeling of confidence that one will get good care establishes a healthy foundation for the future evolution of individuality. But at every or any stage, disruption can occur. Children who do not negotiate the different tasks in the process of creating a self are likely to have an inward feeling that they are without an emotional country, displaced persons, "transitional persons," attached or adhering to neither self nor others, but somehow floating between them.

Complicated though the dynamic and developmental considerations may be (and I have by no means taken them all up here), I can still, without oversimplifying, assert some important propositions about the development of fictive personality.

It is a developmental process, and it is most likely to take shape at certain specific transitional times, when the self is reorganizing toward itself and others, and is slightly disconnected from both normal narcissism (love of self) and the object world (love of others).

Loss or some severe damage to self-affirmation must occur for serious pathology to appear. Brief disillusionment is inevitable in every life. No mother is perfect, no environment completely supportive. Perfect attunement would not prepare the child for the world. When brief disillusion occurs and the child is able to cope with it and find a means of recovering from it, creativity has its beginnings.

Disillusion that is sharply surprising, prolonged or repeated until the self's ability to rebound is crushed can produce a need to find a new self. In some sense, no one wholly succeeds in surmounting all the threats to the self, just as no one fails to overcome many disillusions and to build upon them. Everyone rejoices in fictions. Everyone, at some level, fears that he or she may be a fiction. Fictions can make the self feel isolated, locked in a game. But fictions also allow us to put ourselves in the "place" of others, and thus play a part in the development of empathy, the origins of moral character ("doing unto others") and cooperation with classmates, teammates, and partners.

Early disruptions in the self can be covered over and may not appear at all thereafter. This is normal development and a sign of good defenses. But not all losses are permanently absorbed. Some leave scars or lesions that can tear apart under a new strain. They may be brought forward—sometimes dramatically, sometimes in a slowly accumulating man-

ner—at the oedipal period, in adolescence, in young adulthood, at middle age, or even (as in the case of Don Quixote)
when one passes into old age.

The choice of fictions will reflect—and in treatment dramatically reveal—the internal structure of the self. Thus,
while fictions do not provide diagnoses, they do provide
maps by which to chart the inner life. When did the blow
to self come? It may be shown in the kind of fictional adaptation at one stage or another of childhood. What are the
components and proportions of aggression or affection in
the self?—this can be suggested by the content of the fictive
identifications. Such observations are well known to many
child analysts, who encourage children to play games in
order to give expression to their inner worlds.

Certainly, fictive personality processes are more likely to
emerge within certain personality orientations than in others.
They appear frequently in "as if," borderline, schizoid, and
passive-aggressive schizophrenic types. They have definite
links to the perversions.

These processes may indicate a profound disturbance in
the self; or may also indicate the development of a defense
against regression and the beginning of a movement toward
the restoration of the self. They can provide opportunities
for growth, good growth, or misdirected growth. They have
both defensive and dissociative potentialities, and these must
be judged by the context, not the mere fact, of their appearance.

Finally, if we are going to understand the nature and
mechanisms of the self—whether through classical analysis,
Kohutian analysis, Jungian theory, existentialism, literature,
history, or contemporary social criticism—it is important
to understand the presence, operations, and implications
of fictive processes. They are ubiquitous, and to miss
their presence is to lose a part of the puzzle and mystery
of life.

In psychiatric literature, even in the most recent diagnostic manual, a syndrome is described that dramatically exhibits one aspect of the pathological developmental features of fictive personality processes. This is known as Munchausen's syndrome. The very fact that a mental disorder should have been named after a literary character shows how psychology has recognized the relevancy of fictions in mental operations.

Baron von Münchhausen was a real eighteenth-century person who became a fictional hero in a series of nineteenth-century tales written by Rudolph Erich Raspe. In these stories, the baron is a jovial confidence man, a consummate tall-tale teller, and imposter. The baron is a well-known symbol in world literature for a convincing but harmless storyteller.

Munchausen-syndrome patients are most often found in hospitals. Indeed, they tend to wander from one hospital to another, consulting one physician after another. They tell elaborate, convincing stories about their physical illnesses; these are often so plausible that they are able to obtain multiple hospitalizations. For the most part, treatment culminates in surgery. It often becomes apparent after the operations that the surgeries were unnecessary. Then the true intention of these patients becomes clear. Almost invariably, during childhood, they received abusive treatment from their mothers. In their continuing (often unconscious) rage at their mothers, they seek out new caretakers, physician-"mothers," and convince them to perform unnecessary—and therefore hurtful—operations. Then, the new "mother" repeats the old abuse; he or she is exposed as hurtful when the surgery proves unnecessary. The patient gains a victory over the physician that could not be gained over the original mother. The patient expresses rage at the original mother by tricking the new caretaker into actions that seem like the old abuse.

This syndrome was not identified until 1951, when Richard Asher described it and gave it its name. That other clinicians accepted both the description and the name indicates that it clicked with them. They had seen many patients who played parts and told tall tales as persuasively as Baron Münchhausen had. The presentations of such patients are invariably dramatic and puzzling, even bizarre and inconsistent. They seem eager for attention and they enthusiastically submit to painful procedures; they go from one hospital to another as if existence between hospitals is empty. They show every sign of seeing themselves as central actors in a drama, with the hospital as the stage and the doctors and nurses as supernumerary players. The way that Munchausen cases have been reported in the literature also suggests that the medical authors themselves are uncomfortable, even resentful, at being forced into a drama in which the patient is the main actor and stage manager. One psychiatrist was impelled to compare Munchausen patients to characters in Pirandello's plays, who "find themselves locked in a blurred play where real life and acting are indistinguishable." "True," he said of the Munchausen character, "he knows when he is 'acting' (unlike the hysteric), but even with this knowledge *he can not stop acting*." Another psychiatrist speaks of the physician as providing "a good audience" for these patients.

Munchausen patients use fictions creatively, but it is a special form of perverse creation played out inside the theater of body organs; its perversity is not different from that described in the novels of the Marquis de Sade. In the world of Munchausen, healthy patients are ill; doctors are torturers and killers; mothers are monsters; a lie is a truth—and fictions are used with the utmost creativity for destructive, decreative purposes. Instead of being productive, this sort of creativity empties the body of its organs, one by one, until creativity leads to death.

The standard description of Munchausen patients is tied up with play-acting so as to achieve hurtful, apparently sadistic treatment at the hands of surgeons. But there are also patients who seek out bad psychiatric treatments, and who wander from one mental facility to another, or one psychiatrist to another, making bizarre and often disordered presentations of mental illness. Often they are accepted into psychiatric hospitals or committed to in-patient wards. Invariably, they will tantalize the practitioner with every symptom in the book—anxiety, depression, suicidal thoughts, psychophysiological symptoms, sexual perversions, multiple personality, splitting, and so on. Sometimes they will demand—and get—excessive medications, involuntary commitments to the locked ward, and abuse or coercion from nurses or orderlies or conservators. They may be successful in getting shock treatments or the use of restraints upon them. Then, when they have accomplished the worst treatment they can receive, their symptoms will clear up, and they will seem normal. This allows them to heap blame on one and all, to threaten lawsuits, to "expose" the caretakers to other physicians in the community, and so on.

One such patient, Victoria, was a mother of several young children, when she began to complain of a large number of psychological symptoms. Her husband, an attorney, was able to regulate his own time, and aided by an array of baby-sitters, family members, and helpers, he soon replaced Victoria as the primary caretaker or manager of their children's lives. Victoria's complaints, meanwhile, took a bizarre turn. She had, she said, lived many lives before, and she got "flashes" of them. She revelled in these lives. She was careful not to claim that she had been a very famous person, but her lives were always lived close to the great. She had been, she thought, an attendant to Cleopatra, and had died, along with her queen, from the bite of an asp pressed to her breast. She had even been a writer once, she said, but her books had remained in manuscript, and her poems were never published. Her poems, she said, were like Sylvia Plath's, and she actually gave some creditable examples to prove her point. She had an astonishing imitative faculty. Always her lives ended badly, in pain and misery or mistreatment.

Victoria's medical history showed that during her late teens and early adulthood she had had several surgeries, though their necessity was questionable. She had demanded a cesarean operation when she gave birth. Now she demanded that her therapist find a suitable psychiatric facility for her. No facility in her home state satisfied her, and eventually she chose a hospital over two thousand miles away. Once there, she complained bitterly that the doctors had separated her from her children and husband, that they were depleting her financial resources, and that they gave her no help. During therapeutic sessions she spent the time talking in detail about her past lives. The therapist had to know all about these, she insisted, or how else could he know her?

Victoria used the psychiatric hospital as a theater, the physicians as an audience, and her accounts of reincarnation in order to play out the internal drama of her victimization (as she saw it) at the hands of her parents. Whenever the drama lost some of its "edge," she threatened suicide, ran away, or found some other means of focusing attention back on herself.

Another patient, Tim, under the pressure of traumatic stress from what used to be called "war neurosis," revealed an earlier deficiency in the self that had been covered over by the defensive use of fictions. The last of a large family of children, Tim was born four years after his next older sibling. All of his brothers and sisters achieved considerable success, at school and in business enterprises. Only Tim seemed unable, from a very early age, to "make contact."

When Tim was about one year old, during World War II, his father, a career officer in the air force, was sent into combat overseas. A year later, Tim's mother was killed in an automobile accident. Several weeks passed before Tim's father was able to return home from duty; in the meantime, Tim was taken care of by a variety of friends and relatives. To his father he seemed listless and withdrawn. In a short period Tim's father arranged to distribute the children among various relatives, and he returned to service. Well before the end of the war, when Tim was four, his father was reported missing in action, his plane having failed to return to base.

Tim was moved around quite a bit. Finally, he found a home with an aunt and uncle who lived in a large city. He was regarded as being no trouble. Quiet and withdrawn, with a hard shell, he made his way through grammar school without any remarkable events.

During his high school years, Tim made few friends, except for a brief period when he belonged to a street gang. Eventually he quit school, joined the army, and became a paratrooper. A few days after he first parachuted into combat, he became delusional, saying that he had been wounded all over. His delusions passed rapidly, but then he became obsessed with classical mythology, especially with the gods who lived on the heights of Mount Parnassus. This too passed, but what remained was the feeling of having been dropped and a fervent interest in the figure of Icarus, who had flown so high that his wings had melted. He saw innumerable complicated parallels between Icarus and himself, often confusing Icarus with his father Daedalus. He saw himself as having also been "dropped from the heights."

After a medical discharge, Tim lived alone, having little contact with his siblings or relations. He became obsessed with simply collecting things—or so it seemed at first. But the purpose of the collecting soon emerged. With no training in art, he began to make assemblages somewhat resembling those of Joseph Cornell—that is, built around the idea of a box that contained a large number and variety of objects.

The few mementos Tim had from his father—papers,

photos, a cap—were carefully cut up and made to last for many assemblages. Newspaper clippings and photographs of John F. Kennedy appeared frequently. Some reminders of air travel invariably appeared. Tim was able to allow some of these pieces to be exhibited in a show put on in a community arts center. By this time he was over forty years old, quite solitary, and his war injuries had left him physically impaired. In many ways he still felt "dropped," and his assemblages were evidence of his inner fragmentation. But from the first he had fallen back upon fictions—of mythology, of divine purpose, of artistic creation—to hold him together. And with therapy, these held.

Having seen how fictions can be an armor against loss, let us consider what can happen when development can become misdevelopment when it is suffused with fictions. This was the case with Peter, a young patient whose parents were both well-educated professional people. He was their first child. Around the age of one, Peter experienced two important changes. His family moved from an apartment to a house, and his mother went to work while Peter was left with a sitter. Shortly after this, Peter began to have sleep disturbances. A year later, the house was sold, and the family moved again. Somewhat more than a year and a half later, the family moved a long distance, taking three weeks to go by car. Peter said he was afraid to play outside his new home and began to watch television, especially cartoon shows, for more than four hours each day. He saw *Pinocchio* and *The Wizard of Oz*.

When Peter was four his mother gave birth to another boy. Shortly afterward, the family moved again. During the trip by car, Peter suffered injury to his penis when a toilet seat fell and hit him. The next autumn, at age five, Peter was sent to kindergarten. At this time, his father went on a business trip, and his mother became ill with the flu.

To keep the boy amused, his uncle took him to a magic and marionette show where he met the principal actress and narrator, the "Magic Lady," who was a friend of his uncle's. Three days later, Peter's father arrived home at 2:00 A.M. Two hours later the little boy woke in terror.

His main fear was that he was going to be taken away into a magic land where he would become an unreal, "pretend" being. His mother recorded some of his speech at this time.

> I am a boy, a real boy. I want to go away. Witches are not allowed. The queen, I promised, I promised, I would do it. No. I don't want to be make-believe. I am a boy. Boys don't wear lipstick. Boys don't get flowers. I am my mommy's and daddy's boy. No. Don't get rid of anyone . . . you can't make magic. Don't make my food magic. No, you can't do that. You can't get rid of anyone. Don't get rid of me.

Peter's hallucination records the precise moment in which the person experiences *himself as a hallucination*—when the realm of the self and the world of objects become so tenuous that both become make-believe. Peter is estranged from himself, his food, and his home. He becomes unreal to himself. He struggles against becoming "The Make-Believe." Mommy and Daddy recede into the distance, while the witch prepares to take him to the Land of Make-Believe where everything is changed: boys there wear lipstick, get flowers, and eat magic food.

Obviously, a series of losses and separations occurring just before the onset of these hallucinations revived an earlier fault line in object- and self-relatedness most likely connected with the frequent moves made by the parents and by his mother's return to work during Peter's second year. Seeing *The Wizard of Oz, Pinocchio*, and a magic show shortly before the hallucinations provided a format by which the personality, fragmented and detached from its image of itself as whole and of others as real, could see itself in terms of the available fictions.

It is better, the self seems to say, to be a fiction than to be nothing. Peter's case allows us to see Peter's personality seeking reflections and turning toward fictions; his anxiety shows us how psychotic that moment, internally experienced, must be.

Peter, as he grew up, made a successful but unremarkable adjustment to life. It took him a considerable time in psychoanalysis to work out of his psychotic break and to see himself as he was—simply a vulnerable real boy—separate from his protective fictions. He never again allowed himself to get trapped in a painful inner drama of identifications with fictions created by others. These had saved him, but they had also scared him. And he remained scared.

An opposite example of a person who blossomed through a fiction occurred in the case of Irene, who came into treatment because she was feeling depressed and lonely. A forty-year-old woman whose parents were emigrées from eastern Europe, she had achieved a high-level executive position in a major company. Even so, she felt that her life was empty. These feelings had become overwhelming after she had a hysterectomy a year earlier.

Irene had grown up in an economically and culturally impoverished family in St. Louis. As the fourth of five children, all girls, she had almost no male models or relationships with men. Her father had been killed in an industrial accident when she was two years old, just after the birth of her younger sister. Most of the families of her acquaintance lacked a male caretaker. Living in a world of women, she saw her mother as a very hard worker, and a warm, caring person, but worn-out by overwork and poverty. In an obscure way, Irene felt herself "adopted."

She yearned to make a life of her own, to be self-sufficient—

to "be like a man," as she put it, and thus avoid the abandonment she and her mother had suffered. But where was she to find models for such an independent life? None seemed to exist in her family or her community.

Then, in high school, Irene discovered a series of books whose main characters were independent, self-sustaining, witty women. The first and most important of these was Patrick Dennis's *Auntie Mame*. No wonder this book appealed to her. Not only did it give her a model of a strong woman, but it was the story of an orphan boy who is adopted by his colorful aunt. And so it satisfied both her desire to care for herself and her earlier fantasies about being cared for. Irene took Dennis's book and a series of similar books about feisty heroines as guides, and modeled herself after the fictional characters. The movie of *Auntie Mame* starring Rosalind Russell deepened her identification.

Irene's entire orientation changed. She decided to go to college, gained entrance to a prominent midwestern university, and eventually, achieved a B.S. and M.A. degrees. After securing a good job, she started a successful business career. Quite clearly, her fictional identifications bolstered her development.

Yet she was troubled without knowing why, especially after her surgery. Once she was able to describe in analysis the way she had "imported" her models, a definite pattern emerged. The women in all of Irene's books had been single. Irene too had not married; indeed, she had had almost no sexual experience. Her identifications had apparently made her successful, but at the cost of repressing her sexuality. Also, now that she was no longer able to have a child, her fantasies no longer sustained her. For Mame, a little boy had appeared out of nowhere; but Irene had no prospect of getting a child and thus completing her inner fantasy.

On the surface, she scarcely saw herself as a woman. Although extremely attractive, she regarded herself as unappealing. The identifications that had opened up one source of wholeness for her had frustrated the realization of another aspect of her strivings. At this point, the analysis really began. In Irene's case, fictions had furthered her development, then balked it. But in treatment she was able to resume development of a healthy adult life.

The case of Louis provides another striking example of how fictions can be central to expansion of the personality, especially after trauma has occurred. At the age of five, Louis, apparently a normal, healthy child, witnessed a terrifying incident. He saw his mother and father arguing, and he watched as his mother took a revolver from a drawer, aimed it at his father, and killed him with one shot to the heart.

Louis was taken into protective custody, then within a few hours, placed in the custody of a relative. After a brief time, his mother was released on bail and he was returned to her care. Louis never mentioned the shooting. He did not respond to direct or indirect references to it. In fact, he did not seem to have any memories of his father. He did not seem to dream about his father's death, even indirectly, or to have any dreams at all. He did awaken several times at night, but professed not to be frightened or to feel disturbed.

Others could see that Louis was listless, his play was constrained, and toys did not engage his interest. At times, he suddenly became angry without any apparent cause. Louis seemed to have gotten stuck in a massive repression. The incident of his father's death was like a massive boulder that the stream of his life could not go around.

Several months passed, and there was no change. In therapy, Louis did not respond to suggestions. Nothing interested him. He showed no enthusiasm for play. One day the therapist suggested that Louis draw a picture of "an exciting event," and gave him paper, pencils, and crayons. Louis's father had been a stunt man, and the therapist hoped that in a drawing Louis might begin to deal with his father's life or death. Previous attempts had failed to meet with success, but this time Louis responded. He drew a face, not his father's face, but a heavily disguised one, a clown's face. Then a neck. He drew a racing car around the clown so that only the clown's head and neck were exposed. As he worked on the drawing, Louis became very excited.

Could Louis tell a story about the drawing? the therapist asked. In the rush of his excitement, Louis started right in. The wonderful clown, the wonderful, wonderful clown, who was Louis's "best friend," drove the car with great skill, at very high speed. Everyone cheered. He made the car go "bumpety bump" from one side of the road to another (his father had staggered after being shot), and people screamed with pleasure. But big sharp stones in the road . . . or spikes . . . or knives (here Louis became confused) punctured holes in his tires, and they went bang! and whoosh, the air went out of them, they deflated, and the car stopped.

Louis stopped at that point, confused and troubled, but not knowing why. The clown was all right, he ventured tentatively. "You really wish that your daddy was all right," the therapist said. Louis was silent for a few moments. Then he said, "*Daddy is here*," looked around wildly, and began to cry. That was the impossible fiction that he had to keep secret—that his father lived. But to do so he had had to cover his own life with a veil. Once he exposed his fiction he began to take the veil from his own life and to live again.

Louis's story about the clown, his fiction, restored his development. In time he was able to talk about his few visual memories of the shooting. Then he allowed himself to remember good times with his father. He said that he himself was going to grow up to be a doctor and fix people who were hurt.

# 9

# The Downs and Ups of Creativity

O nce upon a time, in a far country, a boy named Jean was born. He was conceived at a time when his father was ill; in fact, dying. Wasting away with a disease, the father died by slow degrees, and by the time Jean was born, his mother herself was exhausted with fatigue.

Since both parents were virtually "absent" at the time of Jean's birth, he was almost an orphan. His mother tried to nurse him, and was successful for a time. Then her milk dried up, and she sent the baby to a wet nurse.

This was the first of many losses for Jean. Not surprisingly, he was a fussy baby. Furthermore, he soon developed a case of gastroenteritis, and his nurse weaned him early. His care as an infant would seem to have been perfunctory. Then, when he was about one year old, his father died. Jean's mother reclaimed him from the nurse, yet she could

still scarcely care for herself. With her baby she moved back
to her parents' house.

Thus cared for herself, Jean's mother was able to begin
to give her infant good care. He soon recovered from his
early illness, but was troubled by hallucinations and lack
of trust. He slept in the same room with his mother, and
both were treated as children by Jean's grandfather, almost
as if they were brother and sister. Jean had no memories
of his father, except for the photograph that his mother
placed on the wall above his bed and for some marginalia
in his father's books. However, his grandfather doted on
the boy, and Jean was stimulated by the old man's company.
Jean's grandfather, a vain and narcissistic man, played at
looking like Victor Hugo, and he loved to be photographed.
The house was filled with photographs of him.

At age four, Jean began to experience wanting to be like
his grandfather. In external behavior he imitated him perfectly, but internally he knew he was only a pretender.
Though he vowed to be as quiet as his grandfather and
remain perfectly still in church, inside he was troubled by
obsessive thoughts of soiling, of shouting out obscenities,
or urinating in the holy-water basin. He was beset by death-
anxieties and performed numerous compulsive rituals that
would protect him magically. He "had to" cross himself in
a certain way, or hold his body in a certain position in
order to preserve his life. He had a strong feeling of being
an impostor, empty and unreal. He felt himself to be power-
less, yet (like his grandfather) he behaved grandiosely and
treated his mother like a servant. He was, he felt, "a fake
child," lacking a soul, "an object much like a flower in a
pot," "running from imposture to imposture."

At the same time, Jean found the fictions provided by
books and films wonderfully appealing. He became fascinated
by silent movies; at home, alone, he played out all the roles
he had seen on the screen. But there was also something

odd about his identifications, something hollow. His grandmother noticed this and called him a "clown and humbug."
Fictions were too real to him—they gave him his fantasies,
and his fantasies were his life. Because he lived so much in
fictions, he was often alone, silent. He watched silent films,
he read his books quietly. At the age of seven, he decided
to lose the power of speech and remained mute for long
periods.

When he was seven, then, Jean was ready for any available
fiction to offer him an identity or a new role to play. The
disillusions of his early losses seemed too great for the young
self to overcome. But instead, around this same time he
was inspired toward the creative use of his imagination by
his idealized and beloved grandfather, who was real after
all. "He drove me," Jean later wrote, ". . . into a new imposture that changed my life."

Jean's grandfather was an amateur poet. The old man
went on a trip when the boy was eight, and sent his grandson
a letter in verse. The boy replied with a poem. A process
was started. "I received by return mail a poem to my glory;
I replied with a poem. The habit was formed; the grandfather
and his grandson were united by a new bond." Jean was
given La Fontaine's *Fables*. He rewrote them in alexandrines,
a difficult rhythmic scheme. Soon he began to write tales
of adventure. He found he could enter easily into the lives
of others—so long as he himself had created these others—
and that he had a knack for composing tales. He was writing
stories, it turned out, not to escape reality, but as a way of
understanding it. Instead of simply swallowing others' stories
he created his own, and through them he made his way to
reality.

Eventually, writing gave him a role in life and a relation
to others, an audience. It taught him that his own psychic
reality was fundamental, but that he had to account, in his
creations of characters and in the response of his audience,

for the psychic reality of others. At the age of eight, he says, by means of fiction, "I was beginning to find myself. . . . I was escaping from playacting. I was not yet working, but I had already stopped playing . . . by writing I was existing."

All the information about Jean comes from Jean-Paul Sartre's autobiography, *The Words* (1964). In this work, Sartre shows dramatically how isolated he felt as a child, and he gives us enough genetic material to trace these feelings to his early infant deprivations. But he also shows clearly how his capacity for self- and object-relations was restored. Through reillusioning or, in Daniel Stern's phrase, new "affect attunements" with his grandfather, Sartre learned a productive activity that became creativity of the highest kind.

In the work produced by Sartre as an adult the original wounds in infancy are still evident, though they are reworked and richly transformed. Sartre was the first writer to define the philosophy of existentialism, with its emphasis on the imaginary as the core of choice, in his 1945 lecture "L'Existentialisme est un Humanisme." He also dramatized his attitude in the novel *Nausea*, with its portrait of a character empty at the core. Both his philosophy and his fiction suggest that Jean-Paul's early experiences persisted in the work of the adult Sartre.

In very simple terms, the existential quest, as Sartre outlined it, begins with the individual's journey into himself. As he clears his mind of ordinary social concerns, along with past knowledge, memory, and sensations, the existentialist seeker sees a formless chasm inside himself. Does he have no center? It seems so. Looking inside himself, he finds "nothing," a kind of schizoid emptiness. He exists, it is true. But looking back, before his birth, or ahead, beyond his death, the void looms. If existential man, Sartre argues, can focus the powers of his attention on what Sartre terms this core of nothingness, he can transform it into meaning—

the concept of nothingness—which can become a fundamental reality for him. If he must despair over his recognition of the nothing, he can also achieve integrity or courage in conceiving of his being in the context of nothingness. In the concept of nothingness lies the possibility of acting freely. Through his acts he creates his own essence and the character of a provisional reality. Each one of our acts, Sartre argues, creates "the man that we would like to be ourselves," as well as "an image of the man such as we think he ought to be."

This is basically a theory of fictions. When nothing exists, man can achieve meaning by acting "as if" meaning did exist. Revealed in the theory is the very structure of Sartre's own autobiography. When he learned that by creating fictions he could exist, then he became real, in his creativity, to himself. Through his own activity he achieved a reality that no one else could give him. By making literary fictions in a shapeless universe, he found a shape and gave shapes to the world. "Reflecting" is bondage, but creating leads to freedom.

The situation and dynamics described in Sartre's existential theory and in the structure of his autobiography also appear in all his early literary works, and most clearly in his best novel, *Nausea*. At the beginning of the novel, the main character, Antoine Roquentin, vividly conveys his alienation from nature and internal self, both of which he finds meaningless. There are, as he puts it, no events, no actions, no emotions, no ideas:

> The only thing I can say is that in neither case was there anything which could ordinarily be called an event. Saturday the children were playing ducks and drakes and, like them, I wanted to throw a stone into the sea. Just at that moment I stopped, dropped the stone and left. Probably I looked somewhat foolish or absent-minded, because the children laughed behind my back.
> So much for external things. What has happened inside of

me has not left any clear traces. I saw something which disgusted me, but I no longer know whether it is the sea or the stone. The stone was flat and dry, especially on one side, damp and muddy on the other. I held it by the edges with my fingers wide apart so as not to get them dirty.

Day before yesterday was much more complicated. And there was also this series of coincidences, of *quid-pro-quos* that I can't explain to myself. But I'm not going to spend my time putting all that down on paper. Anyhow, it was certain that I was afraid or had some other feeling of that sort. If I had only known what I was afraid of, I would have made a great step forward.

Sartre described his novel in 1963 as "bien sincèrement," indicating that in Roquentin he had described his own attitudes toward the world.

In subsequent decades, as is well known, Sartre went far beyond the narcissistic, schizoid core of his own childhood and of his early novels and philosophical works, into political commitment. To put it in the terms used by the French psychoanalyst Bela Grunberger in his book *Le Narcissisme*, he moved from a centripetal, self-enclosed, negative narcissism to a centrifugal, object-orientated, positive narcissism. Beginning by understanding himself as a fantasy, he proceeded to gain hold of reality by making fictions. As his career developed, he made connections with his fellow man in political action, toward the aim of radical social change. But that is another story, of a very different Jean.

(As a slight digression, it is interesting to note here that Paul Schrader, who wrote the script of *Taxi Driver*, which so strongly influenced John Hinckley, said, "Before I sat down to write *Taxi Driver*, "I reread Sartre's *Nausea* because I saw the script as an attempt to take the European existential hero—from *The Stranger*, *Notes from Underground*, *Nausea*, etc.—and put him in an American context. Travis's problem is the same as the existential hero's—that is, should I exist?

But Travis doesn't understand that this is his problem—so the self-destructive impulse, instead of being inner-directed . . . becomes outer-directed.")

Sartre himself was more fortunate. Feeling empty, he produced imaginary beings. He created what he lacked, and thereby discovered that he possessed a great deal. His childhood entrapment in fictions was a powerful factor in his release into creativity.

In another country, in nineteenth-century California, a boy was born who was destined to be a great general. His name was George S. Patton. As a general, he constructed an entire world of social relations in order to mask—to others and to himself—deep feelings of inadequacy. When Patton was a child, it was soon noticed that there was something different about "Georgie": it took him a long time to learn to read. In fact, he had trouble learning anything. He had to read things over many times to be sure he had understood what he was reading. He found it difficult to write, and could not seem to learn how to spell. He was unable to sit still for long, and his concentration was poor. Today we would call George's problems "dyslexia" and "attention-deficit disorder." Though there were different names for these problems then, his parents and physicians acted quickly to remedy them, at least by removing George from occasions of humiliation. He was taken out of school and received individual attention at home.

Patton's learning disabilities left him unsure of himself in any learning situation, and always seeking to compensate by superiority in other areas, such as vigorous outdoor exercise. Sometimes he exhibited a bravado that put him at risk of real physical danger. His dyslexia was still evident when he was in college. He also suffered from panic attacks and allergies whenever he had to take a test.

Apparently, Patton's father and mother presented him

with appropriate models for success, primarily members of his own family, who had come from Virginia. Most of the male Pattons had been military men. Many had commanded in the Civil War, or, even earlier, in the Revolutionary War. The forebear for whom George was named graduated from the Virginia Military Institute in 1852 and rose to a colonelcy before he was killed at the head of his troops during an attack on Washington, D.C., in 1864. These powerful ancestors, the dyslexic boy felt, had achieved distinction for leadership and personal courage. *They* had not experienced the taunts of students and the disappointments of teachers. If *they* knew how to read, it was perhaps their least important skill. All of these men were virtuous, courteous, brave, vigorous, efficient fighting men—in short, perfect models for George as a boy. He pledged that he would be just like them, even if that meant extraordinary efforts. He *had* to learn to read and write (though years later, the man who became known as General "Blood and Guts" Patton was himself still writing this phrase "blood and gutts"!). He *had* to learn to focus his attention (in order to receive and understand battle reports clearly). He *had* to learn to mask feelings of weakness (so as to inspire confidence in his men). He *had* to learn to take criticism (a commander was tough; Patton initially had to force himself to speak profanely). He *had* to overcome his shyness, and *had* to bend every effort toward making himself speak in public. In short, he had to remake himself.

In addition to the identifications that he developed with a large number of dead military heroes in the family, and from the books his father chose for him (often reading these books to him), Patton added his own group of warriors. His favorites appeared in Walter Scott's novels, in *The Iliad* and *The Odyssey*, in Shakespeare's tragedies, in the Old Testament, and in the books of Kipling. All provided him with a strong masculine model. There was little distinction in his mind among his own legendary ancestors, literary epics, and history. Just as he remembered stories of his forebears, so he memorized long passages from various literary works. (In Patton, memorizing came before and instead of the ability to read. Years later he could still recite stirring passages relating to military heroism.) These books had a special meaning for him. Patton's biographer, Martin Blumenson, writes:

> The stories had a strong impact. They induced in him a strain of mysticism, a sense of dejà vu, and acceptance of telepathy, and a belief in reincarnation, the feeling that he had lived before in other historical periods, always a soldier—a Greek hoplite, a Roman legionnaire, a cavalryman with Belisarius, a highlander with the House of Stuart, a trooper with Napoleon and Murat.

All of Patton's personal fictions and identifications proceeded along this one military-heroic model; nothing else counted. The heroes he most admired were Hannibal, because of his personal courage; and Julius Caesar and Napoleon, for their skills as leaders, their personal courage, and their audacity.

From all of these, Patton transformed "Georgie" into General George Smith Patton. In the process, he developed a fine sense of the theatrical. His military actions were deliberately organized as scenarios. He wrote that "the leader must be an actor" and is "unconvincing unless he lives his part." All his life he honed his personal image, developing what he felt were the appropriate mannerisms—profanity in language, aristocratic bearing, a contemptuous scowl, ruthlessness. For long hours he practiced before a mirror to achieve fierce facial expressions. He spoke often about "my destiny," and became well known for his theatrical displays. With his pearl-handled revolvers and leather jacket, he cut a flamboyant military figure. He flew into well-publicized fits of anger at soldiers who lacked the fighting spirit. He made brilliant use of public relations media. He was grandiloquent and grandiose.

During World War II Patton swore that he could actually smell the sweat of Caesar's legionnaires, for he had been one of them, he maintained, on this or that very spot. Patton relied on such identifications to provide him with a stable inner image of success and he used his concept of destiny to conceal his partly conscious anguish that, after all, he might be weak, deficient, and purposeless. He succeeded in keeping up a constant parallel between himself and his heroes. And behind these he hid the dyslexic boy who dreamed of becoming powerful.

In another far country, Russia before the Revolution, a boy was born into considerable luxury—and a highly neurotic family. Eventually, his own neurotic symptoms all but disabled him, and he travelled to Vienna to receive treatment from the founder of a new science, psychoanalysis. Soon he told Herr Professor Dr. Freud a remarkable dream about seeing "six or seven . . . white wolves sitting on the big walnut tree" outside his bedroom window. From Freud's famous case report centering upon this dream, the young man became known to history as the "Wolf Man," just as if he were not a real person but a fictional or mythical character.

Freud's specification of the details of the case is well known; I am interested here not in the Wolf Man's cure but in his later collapse, followed by a new restoration of his self. About Freud's conduct of the case let me say only that he restored the young man to health by grasping the importance of fictions in his psyche and developing a new set of more usable fictions with him in the analysis. The whole case puts central emphasis on fictions. Tales concerning wolves collected by the Grimm brothers, and found in Russian literature, Jules Verne's novels, *Uncle Tom's Cabin*, legends of Charlemagne,

French romances, and the Bible all recur in the case. "*Don Quixote*," the patient says, "made a tremendous impression on me," and the main character became "dear to my heart."

No wonder!—the Wolf Man *was* another heir of Don Quixote: he too suffered from the disorder and grief, without the benefits, of fictive personality. During the years 1910 to 1914 Freud conducted the case to a successful completion by attending as closely as possible to the Wolf Man's fictions. Freud did what Roy Schafer says all analysts do: with his patient he made new sense of his past and disburdened him for the future by working out with him a new, functional narrative understanding of his life. Together, in Vaihinger's sense, they made a "true fiction."

Then, in 1926, Otto Rank wrote his *Technique of Psychoanalysis: The Analytic Situation*, in which he argued that Freud had perhaps misrepresented, and certainly misunderstood and misinterpreted the famous wolf dream. Freud's ally, Sándor Ferenczi, asked Freud to give him material to counter Rank's attack. At this point Freud made his only mistake in the case—but it was a dramatic one! Without giving the matter much thought, it seems, Freud wrote to his patient, asking him to confirm that contrary to a doubt which had been raised, the dream was as reported. He went further, and cast some doubt over his own earlier interpretation by saying that now he wondered if the "true key" to the dream might lie in the Wolf Man's having seen Tchaikovsky's opera *Pique Dame* (*Queen of Spades*) at an early age. So Freud, it must have seemed, had some doubt about the truth of the narrative upon which the Wolf Man relied!

The Wolf Man wrote back in haste, but unequivocally: "I am completely sure in my belief that I dreamed the Wolf-dream precisely as I narrated it to you at the time. I have no reason to doubt the correctness of this memory." Yes, he said, he had seen *Pique Dame*, it was the first opera he had attended. "It is difficult for me to answer whether I saw the opera before I had the dream."

Despite the friendly, assured tone of the patient's letter, events soon proved that doubt, once raised, started a process of refragmentation that brought back the patient's earlier borderline state. The shock to the Wolf Man must have been terrific. He had lost faith in his fiction. Nor did Freud's subsequent behavior contribute to an amelioration of the Wolf Man's worries. True, he gave the patient special attention by promising to arrange free treatment; but he declared that he could not undertake the treatment himself; he would find someone else to see the patient.

The Wolf Man reentered treatment furiously disappointed with Freud and scornful of Freud's referral of Ruth Mack Brunswick, who was, after all, as the Wolf Man saw her, not only a woman but a newer colleague of Freud's, and younger than he himself was. His first dream in this second analysis had to do with gray wolves ranging fiercely behind a wall, and a woman apparently planning to open a door to let them in. This was certainly an explicit mocking of Freud as an old gray deceiving wolf, and also expressed a fear that this inexperienced female analyst would bring injury by encouraging him to unleash his rage.

A good disciple, Brunswick was intent upon reduplicating and confirming Freud's earlier findings and locating fresh primal-scene material to confirm Freud's earlier emphasis on early sexual trauma. She was also intent on completely ridding the Wolf Man of the prime fiction that he and Freud had constructed, namely, that the Wolf Man was a special, "specimen" patient in the history of psychoanalysis. She writes in her modestly titled "Supplement to History of an Infantile Neurosis": "So long as he . . . [maintained] his position as [Freud's] . . . favorite son, it was impossible to make progress in treatment. Through this impenetrable wall one could not attack the chief symptom of the patient's illness. My technique therefore consisted in a concentrated attempt to undermine the patient's idea of himself as the favorite son. . . ." Now that the Wolf Man was robbed of his psychoanalytic fiction that he was a special patient, a new symptom emerged. Freud had focused upon the Wolf Man's castration fears. Now castration anxiety was displaced, and the patient began to concentrate all his complaints upon one obsessional idea: his nose had become irrevocably damaged. He maintained this steadily, even though, as Brunswick states, no visible problem existed.

Ruth Mack Brunswick diagnosed him as "suffering from a hypochondriacal *idée fixe.*" To the Wolf Man the problem was horrendous: "he felt unable to go on living in what he considered his irreparably mutilated state." Brunswick writes of his agitation: "On the street he looked at himself in every shop window; he carried a pocket mirror which he took out to look at every few minutes. . . . He would . . . examine the pores . . . to catch the hole, as it were, in its moment of growth and development. . . . and a moment later begin the process anew. His life was centered on the little mirror in his pocket." In her waiting room, "he walked incessantly up and down the small hall, taking out his mirror and examining his nose in this light and that." His problem started when his nose seemed to disappear as he scratched at a pimple: "Then he went to the mirror and looked at his nose. Where the pimple had been there was now a deep hole. From this moment on, his chief preoccupation was with the thought, will the hole heal? And when? He was now compelled to look at his pocket mirror every few minutes." In his misery he cried out to her: "I can't go on living like this anymore!"

Freud's earlier treatment had revolved around the theme of castration fears, and on the surface the new symptoms reflected a revival of the old problem. When the Wolf Man abruptly lost the identity Freud had given him, he was thrown back on the central issues behind his castration fears: that he had been "cut off" from both self and objects very early. Now, the fiction that rushed in to occupy his empty self was Gogol's story "The Nose," one of the most popular of Russian stories, and one that he had read as a child. Gogol himself, as everyone knew, had been notoriously hypochondriacal. The "symptoms" and bizarre activities described by Ruth Mack Brunswick are precisely those of the hero of "The Nose." The Wolf Man's concerns derive from Gogol's description:

> That morning Collegiate Assessor Kovalev had awakened rather early. He went brrr . . . brrr with his lips as he always did upon waking. . . . He stretched himself and asked his man for the small mirror that stood on his dressing table. He needed it to examine a pimple that had broken out on his nose the day before. But he was bewildered to find that instead of his nose there was nothing but a bare smooth surface. Horrified, he asked for water and rubbed his eyes with a towel. There was no doubt about it: his nose was not there. . . . He called for his clothes and rushed directly to the police inspector.

He rushes from the house to find his nose, but is thwarted:

> And to make things worse, there was not a cab to be seen in the street and he was forced to walk all the way wrapped in his cloak, his face covered with a handkerchief, pretending he was bleeding, and repeating to himself: "Maybe it's just imagination. How could I possibly have lost my nose so stupidly?"

He tells himself and everyone he meets that "without a nose a man is not a man"—it is impossible to live like this!

Brunswick never recognized Gogol's fictional character in the Wolf Man's symptoms, but she was clear about the "fictitious nature of his complaint." And she was certainly right that "the hypochondriacal idea . . . [served] to cloak those of a persecutory nature behind it," exactly as is the case in Gogol's story.

Brunswick admits uncertainty about what finally brought about his cure; she only knew that it occurred spontaneously. But an understanding of fictive personality processes puts us in the position to make a reasonable hypothesis. Brunswick says off-handedly—but significantly—"His final restoration took place suddenly and in an apparently trivial manner. All at once he found that he could read and enjoy novels." He explained that he had regained the ability to identify with both the authors and the heroes of fiction. Far from trivial, this detail says with undeniable clarity that the Wolf Man suddenly had gotten free of the rigid hold of Gogol's story, and was now able to live in a variety of fictions.

The Wolf Man lived a long life, and his treatment held. He even earned part of his living painting pictures of his famous dream of the white wolves. Freud had been right after all!

# 10

# William Faulkner: The Novelist as a Novel

William Faulkner's life offers a superb example of the downs and ups of creativity and its alliance with fictions of all sorts. For most of his youth and early manhood, Faulkner considered himself a fraud. He felt that he was impotent as a person, and that it was necessary to be an imposter. If he was to preserve a sense of self at all, it would have to be as a fiction. Yet, for all of this, Faulkner finally found an authentic self and an original voice, and became, in the opinion of many, America's greatest novelist.

Since Faulkner tried to conceal his early deceptions after he became well-known, it is not easy to get at his origins. Sometimes he acknowledged that the real Faulkner was his youthful ineffectual self. At others, he virtually denied that he had ever been anything but the great novelist; he gave the impression that he had simply leaped full-blown into assurance and accomplishment.

The double view of himself was reflected in his use of two names. Born "William Cuthbert Falkner," he changed his surname to "Faulkner" when he reached maturity. The novelist "William Faulkner" he told Malcolm Cowley, could be described as "a simple skeleton, something like the thing in *Who's Who:* 'I was born (when and where)' ", resided in Oxford, travelled, was educated more or less, hunted, married, "worked at various odd jobs," and was a literary man. The "other, rougher" "Bill Falkner," had his own adventures, lived in Yoknapatawpha, never wrote books, but consorted with gangsters, mulattos, and loose women; he experienced violent rages, passionate sexual impulses, infantile desires for greatness, and deep anxieties; and he dreamed of death— preferably glorious but, if need be, shameful. This was the Faulkner who said he was born of a Negro and an alligator— a vital and voracious creature.

Was "Falkner" or "Faulkner" a disguise? He couldn't quite say. But these two identities would seem to be the two sides of his creativity: the impulsive side, and the shaping side, which was formal, courteous, and controlled. Occasionally, he would have us believe, the two Falkners met, and "Faulkner" would record the strange doings of "Falkner." (William's brother John later adopted the "Faulkner" spelling in imitation of his older brother.)

Two pieces of personal information about William Faulkner's earliest life exist. One is from his brother John's account of their mother's recollections. The other is a record of Faulkner's own earliest memory, heavily disguised by time.

John Faulkner writes that for the first year of his life "Bill . . . had the colic every night. Mother said the only way she could ease him enough to stop his crying was to rock him in a straight chair, the kind you have in the kitchen. The neighbors said the Faulkners were the queerest people they ever knew; they spent all night in the kitchen chopping kindling on the floor."

Here we are on shadowy ground, unsure whether the infant William was in pain or whether some need in Maud Falkner made her want to hold her first born late into the night. All four of the Falkner boys, we do know, had early difficulties in feeding.

A few details in the account are suggestive. For instance, Maud Falkner "rocked" her children in a straight wooden chair, using it as if it were a rocking chair. (The sound of the rocking was like kindling being chopped.) Notwithstanding the discomforts of this position, there is a suggestion of ambivalence about mothering on her part—a commitment to the duty of meeting the infant's needs, rather than softness or tenderness. The image that emerges is of Maud as a reliable but not warm mother, an impression confirmed by later evidence. Faulkner's mother apparently fulfilled her obligations, but there seems little of the mutuality in feeding and playing necessary to nourish the infant's psyche at its source.

William Faulkner's own earliest memory points in the same direction. Clearly it is a screen memory and needs to be deconstructed, then reconstructed. Faulkner says that he remembers being left at the house of his aunt and cousins, Vannye and Natalie. Then, during the night:

> I was suddenly taken with one of those spells of loneliness and nameless sorrow that children suffer, for what or because of what they do not know. And Vannye and Natalie brought me home, with a kerosene lamp. I remember how Vannye's hair looked in the light—like honey. Vannye was impersonal; quite aloof; she was holding the lamp. Natalie was quick and dark. She was touching me. She must have carried me.

"Loneliness and nameless sorrow." Faulkner's beautiful, simple phrasing gives us a vivid insight into the night fears of abandonment of the child who could only weep until he had to be carried home. Faulkner says that this memory occurred at about the age of three, but the very way he remembers being carried points toward much earlier nights of disappointment and hopeless sorrow and his earliest non-verbal associations. The confusing contrast between the women suggests the confused, fused, ambivalent attitudes he held toward mothering and, ultimately, his mother. Was she a "good" mother?—warm, glowing, approving, and sensuous? Or was she aloof, impersonal, quick, and dark? Did she touch him, without being touched emotionally by him? The infant must have wondered, what kind of mother did he really have? Of course, this screen memory also contains a later element of Faulkner's attachments. He did have two "mothers," the light-skinned Maud, and the dark-skinned black woman Caroline Barr, who often carried his little brother Dean the way William—still clearly yearning for mothering—might have wanted her to carry him.

Faulkner's mature attitude toward male-female relations was closely related to this primitive fantasy of hunger and sorrow. Women, he later seems to have felt, did not feed men—they ate them up. Women were hungry, men were starving. Through one of the characters in an early novel, *Mosquitoes*, Faulkner dated the point at which he believed rejection at the hand of woman occurs: "She devours him during the act of conception." This is what his own unconscious fantasies seem to have told him.

Certainly, Faulkner carried into his maturity signs that eating troubled him emotionally. Mealtimes were difficult for him all during his childhood. Even years later, he confessed to his mistress that he didn't want her to see him eat. "People should eat in the privacy of their rooms," he told her, adding that for him "human mastication" was disgusting.

The picture assembled from these cryptic suggestions in infancy and childhood, supported (as we shall see) by later, clearer evidence, shows that Faulkner trusted his mother, relied upon her, and was attached to her, but that his relation to her was regimented and duty-filled rather than warm and loving. Early in his youth, however, three other women came into his life in rapid succession, and he unhesitatingly attached himself to all three.

The first of these was his paternal grandmother Sallie. In 1901 she made a special trip from Ripley, Mississippi, to Oxford, William's residence, due, as the *Oxford Eagle* reported, to "the serious illness of her little grandson, Willie Falkner, of scarlet fever." He was four years old at this time. The special attention of his grandmother must have been particularly welcome, since his brother John had just been born, and this had suddenly deprived Willie of his mother. A little later, another mothering figure arrived, Maud's mother Leila Butler. She came specifically to help take care of John, but in her spare time she played with Willie. In the same year, another mother-figure arrived on the scene to assist Maud. A black woman named Caroline Barr, she immediately became an important member of the family.

Each of these women gave Willie special mothering. Sallie Murry Falkner taught him about his family history, especially about his grandfather, Colonel J. W. T. Falkner. Leila Butler provided an example of artistic creativity. She was an accomplished artist and spent much of her time painting. For William she carved and clothed a nine-inch puppet that he named Patrick O'Leary; he treasured it and played with it for years. Caroline Barr, usually called Mammy Callie, had two special talents: she was affectionate and she was a good storyteller. It was on excursions with Mammy Callie, when William had to compete with his brothers for attention, that he began, his brother Murry recalled, to "tell tales on his own." Murry added: "They were good ones, too. Some of them even stopped Mammy, and she was a past master in the field if ever there was one."

Through these attachments to three mothering figures William kept up trust in the world and began to work out a network of associations which fused oral affection and well-being with his family history, art, and storytelling. For some time he couldn't decide whether he would follow Leila Butler and become an artist, or become a storyteller like Callie Barr. There was the influence of his great-grandfather too, for that man had been a well-known writer in the antebellum South. "I want to be a writer like my great granddaddy," Willie told his third grade teacher.

His great-grandfather may have had special appeal as a model because the boy had no success in attracting his father's admiration. Murry Falkner was a disappointed man and a conspicuously belligerent drunk. He was severe, distant, formal, and reserved with William, his oldest son, treating him more coldly than he did the younger boys. In William's childhood, Murry owned a livery stable—a messy, fragrant, convivial place where Murry and his cronies could relax and drink and talk. "I more or less grew up in my father's livery stable," Faulkner wrote later in life. ". . . I escaped my mother's influence pretty easily." That was almost entirely an expressed wish, for the boy never got close to his father, and never severed his tie to his mother.

Maud and Murry were constantly at war, and William was on Maud's side, though inwardly he bristled at her strict rules. In contrast to Murry, she was clean, neat, parsimonious, conscientious, and stubborn. She did her duty; she demanded that her sons do theirs. "We lived under a strict discipline at home," John remembers. "Mother," William's brother Murry adds, was "an eternal enemy of dirt in any form." She taught her sons that "waste might be the unforgivable sin." Her motto, and one she certainly taught her sons, was "Don't Complain—Don't Explain." A sign proclaiming this hung above the stove. She never complained. Nor should her boys.

When William was a teenager she decided that he was

stoop-shouldered; she immediately ordered braces for him, "Like a corset . . . [with] two padded armholes for Bill's arms . . . the back . . . stiffened with whale-bone and laced crossways with a heavy white cord." Each morning she laced him into his harness; she was the only person allowed to unlace it at day's end.

William must have been divided and confused. If he was at all like his father, he would be the object of his mother's scorn. But if he took his mother's side, he would never be able to attract his father's love. Each feeling must have been attacked by the opposite emotion; every attachment was shaky. Was he to be impulsive "Bill Falkner"? or controlled "William Cuthbert Faulkner"? He must have concluded that since he was both people, he had to conceal himself behind an imposture and become what he believed would bring him the love he wanted. Had Maud and Murry offered an example of a harmonious marriage as proof that these two impulses could be joined naturally and without contradiction, Faulkner would not have so easily concluded that the world was split. But the marriage was filled with tension and division. Whenever he moved toward identifying with either parent, he disappointed one and lost part of himself.

Despondency and inactivity took hold, and by the time Faulkner reached his teens he simply came to a halt, accepting depression and passivity as solutions to his conflicts. He wouldn't go to school, and he refused to work. A job at the University of Mississippi campus post office was eventually secured for him, but he refused to stir from his chair even to sell stamps. "He said he didn't intend to be beholden to every son of a bitch who had two cents."

The only thing he really wanted, it seemed, was to marry a young woman named Estelle Oldham. All the love that he felt had been withheld by other women he expected to get from her. He even tried to *be* like her. He imitated her in every way, adopting her eating habits, her compulsive

neatness, her intellectual interests—reading and painting—
and her love of solitude. Once Faulkner had settled his affections on her they never wavered. He gave her his ring and
promised to marry her when he could afford to support
her. Meantime, he considered himself married to her. Then
suddenly in 1918 Estelle gave him back his ring and announced that she was engaged to a young naval officer. She
soon was married and left Oxford and William Faulkner
behind.

What he saw as Estelle's betrayal made Faulkner so deeply
depressed that it seemed as though he could escape only
through death. Aside from that he considered himself a fake,
with nothing of himself to cling to. From this point on,
Faulkner really felt like an imposter, and became an imposter.
Estelle had married an officer? All right, Faulkner determined
to become an officer. But this was easier said than done.
When he applied for flight training in the United States
Air Force, he was refused "on the humiliating grounds that
he was undereducated and perhaps too short." Soon thereafter he applied to the Canadian Royal Flying Corps. He
thought that flying for the CRAF might obliterate his depression in a flaming crash, since losses in the air were extremely
high in 1918.

In the papers he filled out for the Canadian Royal Air
Force, Faulkner created an elaborate series of fictions. Before
even attempting to enlist in the CRAF, he had prepared a
fictive genealogy for himself and submitted it with his other
papers. His mother, he specified, was from Britain. He listed
his birthplace as Finchley, Middlesex, and his religion as
"Church of England."

Once he began his impostures he couldn't stop. He wrote
to family and friends back in Oxford that he was being
hastily trained for combat. But the war ran out on him,
and armistice was declared before he had a chance to fly.
After four months, his training was over, and he was mus-

tered out of service. He had not seen any action whatsoever.

In his depression, filtered through romantic idealism, Faulkner had the hope he would be killed, but now he was doomed to live. By the time he arrived home from Canada, he affected a limp and soon began to construct an elaborate story about his war injury. He intimated that he had graduated from flight training (he hadn't); that he had flown (he never soloed); that he had seen combat (he did not leave Canada). He let it be known that he had crashed and nearly been killed. After a time in Oxford his limp disappeared, but when he went to New York in 1921 it "reappeared." Again in 1924, it "came back" in New Orleans.

He was in New Orleans trying to write. He did a little writing, and he met several writers, among them Sherwood Anderson. So convincing was his story about his "war injuries" that Anderson actually believed Faulkner suffered from chronic pain, and concluded that his pain was responsible for his excessive drinking. To his limp Faulkner added the story that he had been wounded in the head. He intimated that with a silver plate in his head, he couldn't be expected to live long. These tales were better by far than anything Faulkner wrote during this time. Anderson was so taken in that he based "A Meeting South," a story about a dying alcoholic aviator, upon Faulkner's "experiences." After 1926 Faulkner's limp generally disappeared but if needed, his war stories were always ready to spring to life. As late as 1935 in Hollywood he tried to win a script girl's sympathy— and to seduce her—by murmuring that he had been shot down over France. He told her: "The sterling in my head is worth more than I am down at the Oxford Bank."

Faulkner's stories of injuries, though "untrue," were his real truths. In his relations with women he really had been "shot down" and he ended up maimed. It was as if he *had* died and come back a new person. He changed the spelling of his name, ostensibly as part of the persona he adopted for the Canadian Royal Flying Corps, he acquired a British accent, and cultivated a British appearance. Eventually, he returned to Mississippi with a limp that was meant to class him with heroes. In some ways, he was also replaying the role of his grandfather, who had been wounded in the Mexican War and later served in the Civil War.

Following his return to Oxford, he wrote to Estelle, signing his new name and a made-up military title. He liked to have his photo taken in his uniform or his "trench coat." Certainly, he loved elegant and especially neat clothes. Uniforms of all sorts appealed to him. He "came alive" when he was in costume. At least part of the attraction of military service might have had to do with the uniform he could have made to order. After his return from flying school, he wore his CRFC uniform around Oxford for years. Even as late as the 1950s he frequently donned a hand-tailored, double-breasted, brass-buttoned, and red silk-lined CRFC blue dress jacket.

His personal appearance often appeared odd. He might show up at breakfast wearing a derby or a pink formal hunting jacket. He was extremely neat, but often wore threadbare jackets because in his parsimoniousness he could not bear to dispose of them, and besides, they indicated a contempt for bourgeois convention. He wore his (unearned) pilot's wings even on his scoutmaster's uniform.

Faulkner seemed to feel no guilt over these deceptions. Indeed, he was pathologically addicted to them; they got him the attention and admiration he craved.

The psychoanalyst Harvey Strauss has described Faulkner's emotional position in the early twenties: "Faulkner needed to create a man to be, a self-concept, out of his imagination, using his own family history and [romantic] myths and his own interests and talents. He first needed to make it tangible in the form of the imposture." Perhaps he would have devoted his inventiveness to imposture all of his life, except that quite unexpectedly, he was given a second chance to possess the woman of his dreams.

Estelle Oldham returned to Oxford in January 1927, having filed depositions to obtain a divorce from her husband. Almost at once she and Faulkner began making plans to marry when her divorce was final. Estelle's return seemed to bring Faulkner back to himself. He was about to win a woman, to be a husband, and, since Estelle had two children, to become an instant father. Strikingly, at around the same time, Faulkner received a questionnaire from *Who's Who in America*, and the way he filled out the form suggests a return to his true identity. Faulkner stated now that his name was "Falkner, William (surname originally Faulkner)." This is, as Faulkner's authorized biographer Joseph Blotner says, a "curious reversal," but its meaning is perfectly clear. He had earlier chosen "Faulkner" to represent his difference, even his alienation, from his paternity. He had used the name "Faulkner" in 1918 on his application for cadet training in the Royal Flying Corps. While William Faulkner went to Canada, Bill "Falkner," the original identity, went into hiding. But now Estelle's marriage was undone, and suddenly "Faulkner" became "Falkner." He could start to become himself. While he eventually retained the spelling which he had used for his first two novels, the old Falkner had picked up the novelist's pen and his writing took a special turn.

Prior to this time, Faulkner's writing had been very limited. In his poetry he was extremely imitative, especially of Conrad Aiken and T. S. Eliot. His impulse to write poetry, he said in 1925, was not derived from the self or an individual vision. He wrote, he said, "for the purpose of furthering various philanderings in which I was engaged"; and to "seem 'different' " in a small town.

His early novels, *Soldiers' Pay* and *Mosquitoes*, are closer than his poetry to his self, but in their irony they too reflect only a part of his self—the bitter, angry part. He is as imitative of Huxley in his early prose as he was of Eliot in his verse. Had he remained stuck in these narrow channels of literary expression, he would have been known to us today as a clever, minor southern writer of the twenties. But as we know, he became a great writer, a highly original one. And his turning point from imitator to literary master, from a negative, restrained writer to a broadly positive exuberant one coincided with Estelle's return and his recapturing of an old identity.

Whenever a serious novelist abandons a promising project and takes up an entirely new one, there is the possibility that some crucial change lies ahead. After Estelle's return and his renaming of himself, Faulkner abruptly dropped one book (called *Father Abraham* in manuscript) and turned to another. The new work, first titled *Flags in the Dust*, was later edited, cut, and retitled *Sartoris*. This was a seminal work. In this book Faulkner first discovered the roots of his Yoknapatawpha saga and moved in the direction of his great novels. It was in *Flags in the Dust*, he wrote two years later, that he discovered a "touchstone" through attempting "to recreate between the covers of a book the world . . . I was already preparing to lose and regret." In it he would "preserve a kernel or a leaf to indicate the lost forest." This description seems to reflect his own life. He had been prepared to "lose and regret" Estelle, but he was given a chance to "recreate" his relation to her. This gave him back a part of himself that had seemed lost. He suddenly realized too, that to make his work "evocative . . . it must be personal," and he created characters reconciling the ideal with the real, "composed partly from what they were in actual life and partly from what they should have been and were not." He thus regained his optimism—as he put it, he "improved on God"—by restoring a relation to the distant past in which his optimism, and only later his ambivalences, had had their origin.

Unfortunately, after initial enthusiasm, his disappointment with Estelle became apparent. It was really impossible for him to be anything but ambivalent about women. Although he stayed married to Estelle, he could not remain faithful. He sought one woman after another and was dissatisfied in turn with each. Still, Estelle's return to him returned to him his oldest self, and that gave him a new start on writing. The women were often replaced. The dedication to his novels went on and on.

From this point forward Faulkner experienced a personality in his writing that seemed new to him, though it was connected with his oldest self, and he began to make the claim that he was different from his books, that Faulkner, not Falkner, was real. He defended this fiction by personal concealment, and by hiding his earlier deceptions. He accomplished this through isolation and myth-making. His chief myth was that his life didn't count in his work.

But the truth is, clearly, that what he experienced and suffered long before he became an artist created the personality—the original, passionate, time-obsessed, ultimately hopeful life—that the adult retransformed into fiction, thereby making the reinstatement of his fundamental powers available and restorative to us.

# II

# Sigmund Freud:
# The Psychoanalyst
# in His Fictions

On April 1, 1884, Sigmund Freud sent his fiancée Martha Bernays a little April Fool's surprise. "Here's a surprise for you. Over and again—I don't know how! Many stories have come into my mind, and one of them—a tale in an oriental guise—has recently taken a pretty definite shape. You will be astonished to hear that I am becoming aware of literary stirrings when previously I could not have imagined anything further from my mind. Shall I write the thing down, or would it embarrass you to read it? If I do so, it will be only for you. . . . I believe that if the train of thought comes back it will really get done by itself. In that event I will write it, and you will chuckle to yourself without saying a word about it to anyone."

So far as we know, the train of thought did not return, or Freud did not write it down. But an inner feeling that early on his mind had shaped itself to fiction stayed with him. A decade later, commenting on the case histories that he presented in *Studies on Hysteria* (1895), he wrote: "I was trained to employ local diagnoses and electro-prognosis, and it still strikes me as strange that the case histories I write should read like short stories and that, as one might say, they lack the serious stamp of science. . . . The fact is that local diagnosis and electrical reactions lead nowhere in the study of hysteria, whereas a detailed description of mental processes such as we are accustomed to find in the works of imaginative writers enables me, with the use of a few psychological formulas, to obtain at least some kind of insight into the course of that affliction." Freud returned to the same theme in 1914 when he told the painter Herman Struck that he considered his work on Leonardo da Vinci to be a "psychobiographic reconstruction" or a *"Romandichtung"*— which is to say, a poetic novel.

Freud has long been acknowledged as a master of prose. But only fairly recently have we recognized how thoroughly saturated Freud's prose is with the strategies of fiction. The literary critic Steven Marcus argued persuasively that in his major clinical cases Freud used the same methods of presentation as did the major novelists of his time. As recently as 1985, the psychoanalyst Harry Trosman has succinctly written, "When Freud wrote about scientific matters, literary models guided his pen . . . he could not have given shape to psychoanalysis without capitalizing on his artistic leanings."

Freud's official biographer, Ernest Jones, speculates that Freud's intense, lifelong interest in the problems of identity— including his obsession with the authorship of Shakespeare's plays—reveals that in adult life Freud continued to experience the derivatives of an early "family romance" fantasy. Indeed, even in later life, he remembered the conscious wish to have been born to his father's brother Josef since his life would have been easier. He fantasized not only that he might be his uncle's child, but the child of nobility. Late in his adult writings Freud reduplicated this youthful fantasy in *Moses and Monotheism*, with the thesis that Moses was not a Jew but an Egyptian of noble birth, son of the Egyptian princess who claimed to have adopted him. Dispossessed of his rightful position, Moses, Freud argued, created a "people" of his own from a group of uncultivated Hebrew immigrants, and taught them the lofty religious beliefs so important to him. Freud explicitly indicated how strongly he identified with Moses; as the "father" of psychoanalysis he too gave new truths to the world, especially by leading his people along— Freud's phrase—"the royal road" to the new land of the unconscious. He saw himself as Moses, but now a Moses who was a Jew bringing a new interpretation of life—psychoanalysis—to a non-Jewish world.

Fictions were a constant feature of Freud's thought—indeed, of his very way of thinking. He also interpreted himself through the figure of Oedipus answering the riddle of the Sphinx, through Joseph in the *Old Testament*, and many other personages from literature and mythology.

Such identifications were not merely casual. Freud's chief way of getting to know himself was through the fictions he discovered inside himself. For a long time, as Freud told Martha Bernays, he had not been aware of these processes that were so crucial to his personality—they had been *repressed*, as he would teach us to say. Then an event occurred that released the fictions.

Freud's father died in October 1896. It is well known that the event had a tremendous impact on Freud. The death, as he told Wilhelm Fliess, had "torn [him] up by the roots"; "I believe I am in a cocoon, and heaven knows what sort of creature will emerge from it." What emerged, of course, was Freud's great book *The Interpretation of Dreams*, the central work in the founding of psychoanalysis, with its strong emphasis upon the influence of the father through the "Oedipus complex." More personally, the book does indeed show that Freud had been torn up by the roots by the death of his father, and that this led to his investigation of his own dreams. Clearly, in trying to find some new foundation for his personality and some new orientation for his life's work, Freud looked toward literature and—beneath literary models—toward fictive processes themselves. Having lost his moorings through the death of his father and the developments in his career that were already separating him from such father figures as Josef Breuer, Freud sought new moorings. Ernest Jones was certainly correct in seeing the fiction of the Family Romance at the core of Freud's early and continuing fantasy life. By a very natural process, then, once Freud lost his first father, he was to seek out other fathers—more noble, more refined, more sensitive fathers—in Oedipus, Hamlet, Werther, and so on.

*The Interpretation of Dreams* is written with the masterly skills of the novelist, for Freud's mind naturally organized itself according to the principles of storytelling practiced by the novelists of his time. As he had told Martha, his stories seemed to take on a shape of their own. In his interpretation of his own dreams, he sees dreams as fictions that identify him; and he explores and analyzes those dreams through the fictive identifications that he finds in them. Moreover, as an instrument for dream interpretation, he discovers a method—that of free association—that is most likely to release from repression the hidden, otherwise disavowed, fantasies of the self.

Dreams, as Freud understood them, are equivalent to roles that we play each night, guises and disguises that we assume in the theater of sleep. They provide the royal highway by which we arrive at an accurate picture of ourselves. The way that we construct our dreams tells the truth about our secret—which is to say, fictional—selves. Understanding of these selves, Freud assumes, can be furthered by the natural correspondence between our unconscious selves and fictions. In *Theaters of the Mind*, a book discussed in an earlier chapter, Joyce McDougall succinctly restated this basic assumption of Freud's when she says: "It is important to recognize within oneself the roles of Oedipus, Jocasta, Laius, Antigone, Narcissus, Hermaphrodite, and some of the sinister furies." According to Freud, it is the "dream person" who needs to be restored to conscious awareness so that the self can achieve integration and wholeness. Each night, freshly, we try on the role of that dream person; then, if we can remember our performance we can make the dream person available to our waking person. The roles of the dream person derive from drives, instincts, early experiences, primitive fantasies, the structure of object relations, myths, novels, theater, mass media, poems, rituals, abandoned identifications, old wishes, ancient beliefs, and so on. The French psychoanalyst J. L. Pontalis describes this well when he says that one purpose of the dream is to be "a staging, a 'private theatre' that provides a permutation of roles [while] allowing one to assume none of them" permanently.

It must be remembered that the dreams that Freud analyzes in *The Interpretation of Dreams* were very often his own. He gives us his own previous associations at the time of the dream, along with new associations that occur to him as he writes about the dream. Thus, in addition to its legitimate and real scientific claims, *The Interpretation of Dreams* is an autobiography of Freud's inner life, a drama of the fictions that shaped his mind, took hold of his dreams, and strongly influenced psychoanalysis. In order to inspect Freud's inner life, we can do no better than to turn to the first dream in his book.

"I shall proceed to choose out one of my own dreams and demonstrate upon it my method of interpretation," Freud boldly remarks, as he dives into an exposition of his theory.

". . . I must ask the reader to make my interests his own for quite a while, and to plunge, along with me, into the minutest details of my life. . . ."

The first dream in *The Interpretation of Dreams* has come to be called the "specimen dream," or the dream of Irma's injection. It was also, in fact, the first of his own dreams that Freud subjected to a detailed examination. Therefore, his use of this dream as the first exemplary dream in his book has a strong personal determinant and suggests how autobiographical, even in its form, *The Interpretation of Dreams* is.

The dream of Irma's injection begins as Freud, the dreamer, finds himself at a party: *"A large hall—numerous guests, whom we were receiving. Among them was Irma."* He is defensive, filled with angry, guilty feelings toward her, for he at once takes her aside, *"as though to answer her letter and to reproach her for not having accepted my 'solution' yet, I said to her: 'If you still get pains, it's really only your fault.' She replied: 'If you only knew what pains I've got now . . .—it's choking me.'—I was alarmed and looked at her."* [Italics Freud's]

It is important to understand, as Freud's friend Max Schur has shown, that in the background of this dream is Freud's troubled relation with several men. First and most important is that with his correspondent and friend Wilhelm Fliess, a nose and throat surgeon, to whom Freud confided all his earliest hopes, and from whom he received encouragement and appreciation. The fact that Freud had considerable emotional energy invested in Fliess's intelligence and insight helps to explain the conflicts that arose between the two men over the treatment of a young woman named Emma (= Irma). In the spring of 1895 Freud was treating her for hysteria, a disorder that he believed was associated with libidinous impulses. Fliess drew Freud's attention to some extraordinary connections between the turbinal (i.e., nose) bones and the female reproductive organs. Freud saw in those observations a possible "solution" to Emma's hysteria, especially with regard to one of her psychophysiological "conversion" symptoms—nasal hemorrhages. He asked Fliess to come from Berlin to Vienna for a consultation. Fliess examined Emma to determine whether there was a "nasal origin" to her hysterical and somatic symptoms—that is, hysteria expressed psychophysiologically. Fliess recommended surgery of the turbinate bone and one sinus, performed the operation, and returned to Berlin.

The aftermath was a disaster. Emma immediately complained of pain; Freud regarded her complaints as hysterical symptoms. During the following weeks Emma developed a severe infection, followed by a massive hemorrhage containing bone chips. Freud's request that Fliess give him "authoritative" advice was fruitless and local doctors treated Emma. One discovered that Fliess had left a half meter of iodoform gauze in the nasal cavity; upon its removal, Emma went into shock. Freud felt ill because of his disappointment in Fliess, his own shame, his guilty self-accusations, his conflict about wanting to defend Fliess, yet to exonerate the patient from his accusations that her complaints after the operation were yet another sign of hysteria. "So we had done her an injustice," he wrote to Fliess. "She had not been abnormal at all." But he also wanted to be sure that Fliess did not feel that anyone blamed him. It is clear that Freud and others *did* blame him for incompetence. Freud's words to Fliess echo with meanings that contradict the statements themselves. Freud said that he was worried only about: "The fact that this mishap should have happened to you, how you would react to it . . . what others would make of it, how wrong I had been to press you to operate in a foreign city where you couldn't handle the aftercare. . . . Of course, no one blames you in any way, nor do I know why they should. . . . Rest assured that I feel no need to restore my trust in you."

In the Irma dream, clearly, a primary wish is expressed that Irma-Emma, and not Freud, is to blame for her illness: "*If you still get pains, it's really only your fault.*" In the dream, if not in reality, Emma-Irma was to blame after all; the symptoms were hysterical, and neither Freud nor Fliess was wrong. However, the reality principle breaks through: the woman says that she *does* have pains. Now in the dream, just as in reality, Irma is examined by several doctors— first Freud, then Dr. M. (Josef Breuer, Freud's coauthor in *Studies on Hysteria*), then "My friend Otto" (Oskar Rie, Freud's family pediatrician and also a coauthor with Freud of a neurological paper). Again, as with Emma, it is discovered that her complaints are not hysterical. She does indeed have an infection, which has resulted from an injection; "*Not long before, when she was feeling unwell, my friend Otto had given her an injection . . . injections of that sort ought not to be made so thoughtlessly . . . and probably the syringe had not been clean.*"

Any figure corresponding to Fliess is entirely missing from the dream. So Fliess cannot be to blame. Nor is Freud to blame for the damage done to Irma; Otto, instead, is the guilty party—he is not from Berlin, but a Viennese physician. A wish is first fulfilled that Irma is to blame for her symptoms. Then when reality intrudes and this wish is denied, another scenario is constructed by which neither Freud nor his friend Fliess has any responsibility. Moreover, the culprit, a former colleague—not Freud's present collaborator—is the one charged with guilt.

Freud says in his "Preamble" to the dream that in reality Rie (= Otto) had told him that a hysterical former patient of Freud's whom Rie had recently seen was "better, but not quite well." His words "annoyed" Freud, for Freud detected "a reproof" in them. In the dream, it is Freud who gets the chance to turn the tables and to direct an accusation of guilt against Otto. The dream reorders reality in order to fulfill Freud's wishes. Freud's reference to a damaging and thoughtless injection, along with earlier references in the dream to the discovery of scabs on Irma's turbinal bones, evokes yet another secret. In his associations in *Interpretation of Dreams*, Freud comments that these findings reflected his concern about his own state of health at that time, but it was Irma who was sick, and not he:

> I was making frequent use of cocaine at that time to reduce some troublesome nasal swellings, and I had heard a few days earlier that one of my women patients who had followed my example had developed an extensive necrosis of the nasal mucous membrane. I had been the first to recommend the use of cocaine, in 1885, and this recommendation had brought serious reproaches down on me. The misuse of that drug had hastened the death of a dear friend of mine.

The "dear friend" was Ernst Fleischl von Marxow, Freud's immediate superior in the Vienna Physiological Institute and thus he was another of Freud's collaborators. To relieve pain due to repeated surgeries Fleischl had used morphine and soon became addicted. Freud was one of the pioneers of the medical use of cocaine, having published a paper on it in 1884. He recommended to his friend that he make use of cocaine in order to relieve himself of his morphine addiction. Freud states in *The Interpretation of Dreams* that he had recommended only oral use. But Fleischl gave himself cocaine by injection, and as a result, he died. Now the dream, as Freud says in his associations, clearly alludes to the unfortunate fate of Fleischl. Once again, Freud implies, he satisfies the wish for Otto to be responsible for injections that were "thoughtlessly" carried out.

In the center of the dream, Freud refers to another set of collaborators: "My friend Otto was now standing beside the patient and my friend Leopold was examining her . . ." Leopold (Dr. Ludwig Rosenberg) and Otto, he says in his associations, were in the same field and thus "it was their fate to be in competition with each other, and comparisons were constantly being drawn between them."

Beneath the manifest content of the dream, there seems to be a complex web of feelings about competition, along with idealizing and depreciative feelings about the collaborators with whom Freud was in competition—the "disobedient" patient Emma, Fliess, Breuer, Fleischl, Rie, and Rosenberg. The dream is driven, I believe, by Freud's wish always to be right and blameless, as well as the winner in the struggle for supremacy between himself and any other man. This supreme fiction clearly operates throughout the dream. Just as he "should" have been born the son of his uncle—his father's brother-collaborator—so he should achieve victory over his competitive collaborators.

Then suddenly there is an oblique association to a novel. Elaborating on his associations, Freud writes: "Scenes such as the one represented in the dream used often to occur [in the Kassowitz Institute for Children, where Rie and Rosenberg were Freud's assistants]. While I was discussing the diagnosis of a case with Otto, Leopold would be examining the child once more and would make an unexpected contribution to our decision. The difference between their characters was like that between the bailiff Brassig and his friend Karl: one was distinguished for his quickness, while the other was slow but sure."

Freud is referring to a novel by Fritz Reuter (published in 1864 and written in Plattdeutsch) titled *An Old Story of My Farming Days*. This novel concerns the fortunes of a middle-aged farmer named Karl Hawermann, and his friend since childhood, Zachariah Brassig. Reflecting on their schooldays, Brassig makes the statement alluded to in Freud's associations: "Ah, yes, in quickness I had the best of it, but in correctness, you had." At various times in Reuter's book, the two men do collaborate, and at the end, they choose to live together. The hero of the book, however, is

Karl: compared to him Brassig has a distinctly minor role. Freud clearly identified with Karl, the "slow" one. He refers to "Karl" by his familiar name and to the friend by his surname. Certainly, though he associated Leopold and Otto with Karl and Brassig, he himself also identified with Karl, and this identification tells us about Freud's state of mind in 1895, when he had the dream of Irma.

In the book, Karl is at first a failure. Then later, he is given a position of trust by an owner of a large estate and he manages the estate so well that he becomes a great financial success. The owner dies, and his son inherits the property. Then Karl's troubles start. The new owner is jealous of him, disputes his management, and accuses him of thievery. Thanks to Brassig's help, Karl is shown to be innocent, and he lives on the estate, while the owner takes a smaller property. Karl's dilemma in the novel is that he is often mocked as a failure, doubted, criticized, and suspected of a criminal act, though the reader knows that he is an honest, reliable and excellent manager. He is not seen or appreciated for what he is; instead, he is depreciated just where he should be praised. At the end, he is completely cleared of blame; his good qualities are recognized at last.

We already know that Freud was experiencing difficulty in many of his collaborative associations, and in addition was feeling the sting of blame—for Fleischl's death, for Fliess's error, for having clashed with Breuer over the etiology of hysteria. And unconsciously at this time he passed into identification with a character in a novel.

Other identifications reside in this fictional character of Karl Hawermann. Hawermann was poor and, like Freud, had to wait a long time before he could afford marriage; his final success mirrors Freud's wishes for financial success. Hawermann was an honest worker, but was nonetheless falsely accused, castigated, and dispossessed from his position after years of faithful service. Freud seems to have been fearful that this too would happen to him, and psychically Hawermann's vindication implied that Freud too would be justified. The impulse to be cleared of wrong is so strong in the Irma dream that it broke through from underneath to the manifest content: *"I at once called in Dr. M.* [Breuer], *and he repeated the examination and confirmed it."* Indeed, Freud's wish to be cleared of responsibility for Fleischl's death was still so strong, even at the time of writing *The Interpretation of Dreams*, that in his associations he implied that he was opposed to Fleischl's self-administration of the drug by subcutaneous injection, when in fact he had not protested and had even advocated such injections for withdrawal from morphine. Breuer is represented in the dream as a good parent-collaborator figure, whose role is simply to affirm the correctness of Freud's diagnosis. Indeed he is even made to look like Freud's older half-brother Emanuel, who was living in England (like Emanuel, Breuer in the dream is clean-shaven and walks with a limp). The dream wish is that Breuer should be, in short, a brother to Freud, not a potential critic (as he proved to be) of Freud's theories of the sexual etiology of hysteria. In that sense, in the dream Dr. M. (Breuer) functions like Brassig in the novel. Brassig is a double, a "best friend," a schoolmate who is there whenever needed, and he has no real claims of his own.

The dream also shows that Freud, nearly forty, feared that he would never achieve the grand success of which he dreamed: he was experiencing criticism instead, and as a result he was deeply disturbed. He yearned to be rid of all conflict, criticism, guilt, self-accusation, doubts, and fears. He wanted, grandiosely, to be affirmed by the world as right in everything. In his own analysis of the Irma dream, he refers to Fliess as "a person whose agreement I recalled with satisfaction whenever I felt isolated in my opinions. Surely, this friend who played so large a part in my life must appear again elsewhere in these trains of thought." In fact, what Fliess positively represented was a friend who always takes one's side; that constitutes the strongest wish in the dream.

Ultimately, the dream-thoughts elaborate on this idea. Karl's ruin occurs when the owner of the estate where he works as bailiff dies. The owner's son takes his place, and trouble soon develops between Karl and the new squire. The oedipal aspects of this relation are obvious, for the squire's wife admires Karl while the squire suspects him: but beneath the oedipal level is a more fundamental contrast between the good and loving squire-father and the bad, doubting one. The novel and Freud, the dreamer who associated to it, split the parenting figure into two kinds of collaborators, the parent who is an empathetic, mirroring, supportive figure, and the parent who opposes and balks, who does not support self-affirmation.

Freud used the "specimen dream of Irma" in order to illustrate his method of dream analysis. But it also makes a crucial personal claim in its underlying theme. Without knowing *An Old Story of My Farming Days*, certain central features of the specimen dream of Irma's injection remain closed. When we expand what Freud condensed, the dream unfolds to us.

The same conclusion would be arrived at over and over again were we to examine other dreams by Freud: they are all thoroughly suffused by central fictions. Most of us read books, remember them for a while, and then, except for rare works, they become peripheral to our lives. Freud, however, not only remembered a very large number of fictions, he "remembered" them in his unconscious. The founder of psychoanalysis created a science of fictions.

In 1934, near the end of his life, Freud, in a visit from the Italian author Giovanni Papini, took the opportunity to reflect on how he saw his career at its culmination. In a little-known interview he told Papini, "I am a scientist by necessity, and not by vocation. I am really by nature an artist. Ever since childhood, my secret hero has been Goethe. I would have liked to have become a poet, and my whole life long I've wanted to write novels." He told Papini that from the time he went to study with Charcot in Paris (1885–86), he had been interested in the major literary movements of his time; and that these—symbolism, naturalism, and romanticism—were adapted by him to psychoanalytic theory: they were "the inspiration of all my later work."

Freud continued in his explanation. He had, he noted, "carried out the very same plan as Zola." That is, he collected human documents and treated them naturalistically, scientifically. From the Symbolists he was alerted to the importance of dreams and language. From romanticism he learned to stress self and sensibility. Finally, from his own early interest in the classics, he remembered "the myths of Oedipus and Narcissus."

But, he sighed at the end of the interview, "My oldest and strongest desire would be to write real novels, and I possess a mine of first-hand materials which would make the fortune of a hundred novelists. But I am afraid now it would be too late."

# 12

# Fictions
# and Culture

In a traditional society, as Dorothy Lee, an anthropologist who worked with the Wintu Indians of northern California, observed, "the self has no strict bounds, is not named and is not . . . recognized as a separate entity." For example, she says, the Wintu do not use the conjunction "and" to describe two people who are living together; instead of saying "John and I," they will say "John we," describing their unity rather than their separateness. The Wintu have difficulty in talking about a separate self. Lee writes:

> When I asked Sadie Marsh for her autobiography, she told me a story about her first husband, based on hearsay. When I insisted on her own life history, she told me a story which she called, "my story." The first three-quarters of this, approximately, are occupied with the lives of her grandfather, her uncle, and her mother before her birth; finally, she reaches the point

where she was "that which was in my mother's womb," and from then on she speaks of herself, also.

The self, then, is traditionally part of a much larger whole, from which it is only provisionally and indistinctly separated. Lee and other investigators of traditional cultures demonstrate that on the one hand the self merges into the social unit, totemic clan, line of descent, and so on. From another angle, the self also has clear affiliations with nonpersons, and it sometimes merges with spirits, mythical creatures, demigods and gods, monsters, sprites, guardians, totems, and so on. Thus, a personal autobiography is likely to become a history of the family, while this in turn may touch upon the crucial influence of gods and spirits on the family or individuals. Saints, guardian angels, or various intercessors may be watching over the individual and directing his life. This traditional concept of the world is still held by many people, even in technologically advanced societies. Thus the individual has crucial relations with "persons" or "beings" whom he has never seen. This can be understood by anyone who has read *The Iliad* or *The Odyssey*, where history, gods, and men all interact, and people have important relations with many more "people" than those they actually encounter.

Modern society has introduced some new features into this traditional structure, partially replacing elements of tradition, while adding new ones but not altering the structure of tradition as such in social life. All of us have real relations with a limited group of people—family, friends, coworkers, and so on—whom we see more or less frequently and know something about. We know about the doings of our family; we will ask our UPS man about his daughter in college; we will hear, if only occasionally, about the success or failure of a construction business owned by our next-door neighbor; and we will watch children on our street grow up. Those who live in high-rise buildings may not know anything about the neighbors with whom they share walls, ceilings, or floors; but they too will know a good deal about some hundreds of people whose lives they touch. Even when face-to-face relations are infrequent, the use of multi-copied letters, the telephone, and other devices (tape-recorded communications, exchanges of photographs, etc.) facilitate a sort of technologized intimacy. All of these contacts fall into the category of *real social relations*.

However, we now have the illusion of relations with an additional multitude of human beings. Radio brings us call-in shows, talk shows, and gossip programs; we can get therapy, recipes, and gardening tips from people we have never seen, never will see, and know nothing about. Any supermarket is filled with magazines and tabloids with intimate details of the lives of celebrities. Television gives us the rich and famous in domestic glimpses. Whether the setting is actual or a stage set is unclear, and whether the discourse consists of personal revelations or an elaborate script is impossible to know. Various estimates suggest that adults average three hours per day of television viewing. A child entering school has spent thousands of hours watching television. In the earliest years of life, and again in the later decades, engagement with technological illusion is strong. Children and older people often talk to the television. They feel as strongly about fictional characters as about real people. A young woman told one investigator that she had a "special relationship" with TV interviewer Dick Cavett. "She watched his show with interest and involvement; if he said anything which she thought unworthy of his character, she would say, 'Oh, Dick,' in a scolding, impatient tone. Although she has never met the man, her heart is his."

To a large extent, the gods, spirits, monsters, or saints and intercessors of traditional society have been replaced in contemporary society by a conglomeration of beings we have never seen and never will see. Yet we are encouraged to believe we do have some relationships with them. These include public persons; actors and actresses, especially those in soap operas, situation comedies, shows like "Dallas" or "Dynasty," and miniseries; characters in novels; figures in theme parks such as Disneyland; comic-strip characters; and toys. Often, the "real" persons merge with the fictional characters, and we may see an actor who plays a doctor being called upon to give medical advice. Consider also the commercial on TV in which an actor says: "I'm not a doctor, but I play one on television," and then proceeds to give advice about home remedies. We even have a phrase, "TV personality," to describe someone whose existence depends on appearances on television.

A characteristic form of contemporary literature involves this same blurring of actual and fictional existence, as in E. L. Doctorow's *Ragtime*. And when Sigmund Freud meets Sherlock Holmes in Nicholas Meyer's *The Seven-Per-Cent Solution*, some people will not remember that the one existed, while the other did not. (Indeed, numerous letters are still sent to Mr. Sherlock Holmes, 221-B Baker Street, London, England.)

A first novel published in 1982 offers another striking illustration of this blurring, even for the characters themselves. This is Meg Wolitzer's *Sleepwalking*. At Swarthmore College three undergraduates who admire the women poets of the previous generation decide to play a special sort of game. Their favorite poets have all committed suicide—Sylvia Plath, Anne Sexton, and Lucy Ascher. (Plath and Sexton did commit suicide; "Lucy Ascher" is a fictional poet.) Each one of the young women adopts the *persona* of one of the poets. They stay up all night reading the work of these women; they revel in their own melancholy; they don the appropriate costumes, wearing only black. Above all they are serious, depressed, and, except for each other's company, they remain isolated. Around campus, they become known as "The Death Girls." Claire is the name of the undergraduate who identifies with the poet Lucy Ascher.

As the story develops, Claire eventually meets a young man named Julian. He doesn't seem so bad—in fact, her melancholic perspective lifts a bit whenever he is around. He tells her that he "likes" her. She can see that he does. She discovers that she even "likes" him. Suddenly, her obsession with Lucy Ascher seems less appealing. Why be a "death girl" and brood on the darkness of life when life and love seem to offer alternate possibilities? College isn't such a lonely or oppressive place after all. But Claire can't get out of the role of Lucy and back into her own identity as Claire. Her fictions have merged with her personality. How can she exorcise them? Her friends suggest a solution and she takes it. She gets a job at the Ascher's home as an *au pair* girl, she sleeps in Lucy's bed, and she tries on Lucy's clothes. Instead of identifying with the mythologies surrounding Lucy's suicide, she gets a full measure of Lucy's life. She inhabits Lucy's reality, and this breaks the spell of make-believe. Now that she becomes a real girl, she sees that she had been using a perpetual state of mourning as a defense against her own painful family history, with which she now comes to terms. She can risk reality after all. Such a situation as Claire's has become part of the mythology of our time. Fortunately, she manages to pull away from her destructive fiction.

In his book *The Modern Temper*, Joseph Wood Krutch suggested that there have occasionally been times when entire societies have been composed around a prevailing fiction: "Louis XIV," Krutch said, "tried to live as though he were the hero of one of Racine's tragedies; Sir Philip Sidney tried to live as though he were the hero of one of those half-pastoral, half-heroic prose romances of which he gave the world an example; Byron as though he were his own Childe Harold; and all the members of the society of King Charles

II's day as though they were characters in one of Congreve's comedies." Krutch remarks that fiction provides "the various forms toward which various people of various societies have endeavored unsuccessfully to aspire."

But contemporary society has succeeded in imitating fictions on a widespread scale. An anthropologist of contemporary society who carefully drew a description of social relations from his informants would gather that nearly all of us have three sorts of social groups to which we feel an intimate relationship: (1) those whom we see and know; (2) those who are not seen but are a part of traditional belief systems, including gods and ancestors; and (3) those who are never seen and about whom belief is created by various media. The first group, which may number from a few people up to several dozen, is "chosen" by the social reality of actual economic, political, and personal relations. The second group, numbering perhaps one hundred, is "chosen" by exposure to transpersonal belief systems in society or the family. The third is "chosen" by the intersection of personal emotional investment and media availability, and is limited only by that person's consumption of newspapers and magazines, radio, and TV. Any "self" is thus a community of selves, which includes differing internal impulses, along with a vast, contradictory barrage of external stimuli. In a traditional society, there is general agreement about the content of the unseen world. Moreover, there is harmony between the components of the unseen world so far as its genesis, its spirits, and the place of one's ancestors in it are concerned. Harmony exists, too, between actual social relations and those that could be called fictions.

However, this is far from true in contemporary society. In a relatively short period of time, we may play a violent video game, watch a romantic movie, cringe before a caustic comic, read about the domestic crisis of a country-and-western star, laugh at a situation comedy, become engaged with the fate of a TV family, be taken into an alien future, or transported to an equally alien past. The toll on emotions is extraordinary—but, even more important, the competing, conflicting interpretations of the world so experienced makes for continuous internal division. Furthermore, the component of fictive social relations is immeasurably larger in the contemporary self than it has been in the past.

What does this mean for modern men and women? First and foremost, actual social groupings have been overshadowed by social relations that are fictions. As a corollary, personal emotions become attached more strongly to fictions than to people. Participation in the lives of others is replaced more and more by fantasies of others' lives. And finally, since fantasies and constellations of fictional identifications are individual, the perspectives we share with others become more and more limited and narrow. Contemporary men and women, then, are less able to distinguish between fictions and actual social relations. Instead, we see people leading lives as if they were characters in romance, adventure, mystery, drama, comedy, tragedy, myth, novels, and advertising.

The cultural anthropologist John L. Caughey has cited a good example of such confusion. After attending a Chicago Cubs baseball game in April 1947, a sixteen-year-old girl developed an intense crush on Chicago first-baseman Eddie Waitkus. She often went to baseball games to see him play, but she never tried to speak to him or get his autograph. She did collect newspaper clippings, photos, and articles about him, and in her room at night she spread these out as "a kind of shrine." She kept one of his pictures under her pillow. Since Waitkus was of Lithuanian descent and came from Boston, she became interested in both. She became obsessed with the number thirty-six because that was his number. To her family and girl friends she spoke romantically about "Eddie." She talked to his pictures, she dreamed of him, and developed fantasies of dating and marrying him.

age eighteen, he will have watched 17,040 hours of TV and seen 15,000 murders. Another statistic is put this way: "Three-year-olds watch an average of forty-five minutes a day, five-year-olds watch two hours a day, and children older than five spend four hours each day watching TV. Every day, all across America, children younger than twelve spend a total of 70 million hours glued to the set." An average of five acts of violence occur per prime-time hour, but on the weekend twenty violent acts are seen per hour on daytime children's programs.

The high level of aggression on television scarcely requires elaboration, nor is the power of television to attract attention at question. Surveys since the 1960s show that mass communications command more of a child's waking attention than any other activity, including school. In the movie *Poltergeist*, the young girl played by actress Drew Barrymore sits raptly in front of the TV set even though the programming has gone off for the night and electronic "snow" fills the screen. Suddenly a ghostly arm reaches out of the screen and pulls the child in! This, of course, is science fiction, but behind it lies the psychological truth about the way television seizes a mind. The child, even the adult, can be pulled through the screen, and then, like Alice, have a hard time getting back out again.

One young patient was pulled into the television set by getting stuck in a movie. George was left alone for long periods since his mother worked, and his grandmother, who was his babysitter, paid little attention to the boy. However, George's grandmother did have a VCR, and George found one film that attracted him. He played it over and over, watching it avidly. Eventually, people who talked to him noticed that his conversation, though voluble, was strained and artificial. Finally, his grandmother realized that George would say no words except those which were uttered on that one videotape. He had every phrase memorized and,

She cried for a whole day after he was traded. Such
relation is part of the experience of many normal adol
in many ways the heir to childish fantasies of im
playmates, twins, and the family romance.

But then, this girl's thoughts took an aggressive tu
as if she and Waitkus had had an actual relationsh
he had treated her badly. Caughey writes that the g

> "After a year went by and I was still crazy abou
> decided to do something about it." She decided to re
> situation by murdering Waitkus; "I knew I would nev
> know him in a normal way, so I kept thinking I will r
> him and if I can't have him nobody else can. And then I
> I would kill him." In June 1949, learning that he was
> there with his team, [the girl] checked into a Chicag
> She talked with him for the first time on the hotel ph
> was "shocked" at the way he spoke), and asked him
> up to her room about "something important." When he
> she pulled out a gun and said, "For two years you ha
> bothering me, and now you are going to die." Then
> him in the stomach. In the uproar which followed
> disappointed and angry that people in neighboring hote
> were so "dumb" that they "didn't know who Eddie
> was."

Starting with the germ of an actual social activity-
to a baseball game with friends—this girl rapidly
into the area of fiction. She loved the athlete and she
to kill him. But she loved an illusion, and the man s
was someone she didn't know at all.

Television, of course, has been the prime instrun
promoting the rapid increase of fictions. In particu
puts heavy stress on aggressive relations. Between th
of five and fourteen, according to media expert Otto I
"the average American child has witnessed the viole
struction of 13,000 human beings on television alon

with great ingenuity, adapted them to all situations as best he could. Eventually, George went into therapy and was able to ease out of his fixed role. Not everyone is so readily released back into the world.

We have read newspaper reports that numerous teenagers have been stabbed or beaten during or immediately following the showing of the gang movie *The Warriors;* that a young man hanged himself after reading an article in *Hustler* describing the sexual ecstasy associated with asphyxia; that another young man committed suicide based on "instructions" he got from a rock record; that after viewing a TV film, *The Burning Bed*, several men and women shot or maimed their spouses; that a street gang burned a woman to death in imitation of a similar event that occurred on a television show. The woman who was burned to death, like the woman on TV, was carrying a red gasoline can. We hear that five Croatian men hijacked a TWA flight in 1976 with one real and several fake bombs, and that one hijacker, as they gave themselves up in Paris, said, "Well, that's show biz!" We read that a man on death row whose appeal was denied said spontaneously, "It's show time!" Only weeks after an aborted skyjacking in 1971 involving a parachute, a copycat skyjacker, D. B. Cooper, actually brought the deed off. During the next week, Cooper's feat was imitated five times; dozens of similar attempts followed. Clearly these were not imitations of Cooper, for little was known about him. They were imitative of the Cooper-of-the-television. Fictions spawned fictions; soon, T-shirts were being sold inscribed "D. B. Cooper, the only way to fly," saloons were named "D. B. Cooper's Place," bowling alleys proclaimed D. B. Cooper sweepstakes, and so on.

Since the publication in 1972 of the "Report of the Surgeon General's Advisory Committee on Television and Behavior," an avalanche of research projects on this subject has been commissioned by the Federal Government and more than three thousand publications have resulted. Of these, the largest number document the effects of the media upon aggression. The original Surgeon General's advisory committee and most of the subsequent researchers concluded that there existed "a causal relationship" between television violence and later aggressive behavior. These studies offer report after report documenting this relation. In a five-year study of 732 children, for instance, conflicts with parents, fighting with peers, and delinquency were all correlated with the total number of hours of television viewing. Two other studies compared aggressiveness in children before and after their communities had television; in both studies, verbal and physical violence increased measurably. The surprising result of these studies and many others is that the fundamental correlation is not between aggressive behavior and the viewing of violence on TV; increase in aggression correlates with *viewing* television, not with viewing violent scenes. The *process* of viewing is the main factor in causing psychic and behavioral change.

Subsidiary findings included correlations between television viewing and decreases in verbal fluency and creativity. Children who watch videos for instruction tend to solve problems only on the basis of facts or concepts presented on the videotape, whereas children who learn the same materials in a traditional manner solve problems more freely and individually. Decrease in cognition tends to occur whether the program viewed is an adventure show, a comedy—or even an educational program. A program whose subject is how to increase creativity is likely to decrease creativity in the viewer. What is more, it is now clear that material derived from mass communications is stored much longer than anyone supposed it would be. This has been proved over and over by how easily people answer trivial questions based on media knowledge. "Material" is simply that, content separated from evaluation, so that TV commercials are remembered for as long a time as the details of a momentous news broadcast. Indeed, repetition rather than intrinsic importance determines how influential material will be.

The very nature of television, as well as the organization of programming, obliterates the line between reality and fiction. The structure of the medium, with one image piled upon another in short sequences, works against effective mental differentiations. No one could guarantee being able to watch any given sequence of television and then being able to state with certainty whether this was news, fantasy, or commercial material. In commenting on the television coverage of the "last stand" of Patty Hearst's SLA kidnappers, Frederick J. Hacker showed the tremendous power of electronic media to erase the distinction between fiction and historical reality:

> Events became socially effective and important through their mass-reproduced image. Often they take place only for the sake of the image; they are produced in order to be reproduced. The image is no longer only the reflection of reality; the image *is* reality, most likely the only one accessible to us. We have to rush home to see and hear what's really going on; the place in front of the television screen is the center of contemporary experience and the observation point of the universe, which is brought into our living room for our edification, stimulation, and entertainment in neatly subdivided pieces. Distinctions between real and fictional violence are blurred; the fiery auto-da-fé in the real ghetto did not look much different from any similar scene staged in a studio. Shown during prime time, it was also just about over in one hour, which is desirable timing for a crime program.

When the medium itself does not distinguish between actuality and fantasy, judgment is diminished, and this allows for the release of offensive, previously censored aggressive impulses. Though books have always inspired identifications, television seems to bypass control of the ego, encouraging unmediated identification with the image. This is exactly what John Hinckley claimed (without any reflection on his own disordered behavior) when he wrote to the editors of *Newsweek:* "Watching too much television can cause numerous social disorders. The damn TV is on all day and night in most homes and is probably more harmful than movies and books. It is not a good way to pass time because, once again, a fantasy world tends to develop the longer a person stays in front of the tube."

Study after study has shown that people of all ages, but particularly children, have difficulty distinguishing what is "real on television," and this has profound consequences for the development of a sense of reality in children. In a 1980 study, researchers found that urban-school and primary-school children accepted what they saw on television as real. Crime and detective stories were most disturbing, while, for instance, westerns were less stressful because they seemed to occur farther away geographically and psychically. Other researchers asked children ranging from kindergarten to the fourth grade to sort out characters who were human, animated, or puppets among those they saw on TV. Kindergarten pupils had trouble doing so. They also failed to understand how television works, making such comments as: the characters "got into the television set because they are smaller than us" or "they're lowered down on a rope." Many of the older children, although they could distinguish between the characters, did not know how cartoon characters are made and animated. These results were confirmed in a study showing that many children had difficulty explaining how characters got into the television set. Some said they entered through the "plug in the wall." Especially under conditions of unsupervised extensive viewing of television, children may come to believe that magical effects can be achieved in real life. Of thirty young children investigated in 1970 and 1973, fourteen believed that a "person" on television had spoken directly to them, and six of the children remembered answering back.

The opposite result of mass communications is the alienating effect upon the consciousness, in which the child gathers that nothing he or she sees, on television or anywhere else, is "really" real. This observation may seem contradictory. But it is the outcome of initially believing everything. Very soon children learn that what they believed was real is only illusion. Television characters do not answer questions, they never address the children directly. Parents tell children not to believe they can fly, that there really is no Superman, that chickens cannot really talk, and so forth. The result is that the child, who may be searching desperately for certainty, gives up the belief that everything in the media is real and instead concludes that *nothing* is real: news broadcasts are just as imaginary as "Sesame Street." Some children thus come to prefer "make-believe." They try to interpret everything as "not what it seems"—in short, they prefer a world from which confusing reality is excluded. Children learn to follow "scripts" rather than test reality, and they are often bitterly disappointed when reality upsets the scripts they have learned. Whether they conclude that "everything is real" or "nothing is real," everything is a fiction. Violence has no consequences, the murdered actors will be seen alive on other shows.

The great German writer Ernst Jünger, reflecting on the First World War, came to the conclusion that the mechanical terrorization of that war had driven people into regressive mental positions. Jünger postulated that men, women, and children who experienced warfare were sent into a remote state of mind which he called a "second, colder consciousness," in which personal acts and experiences of events were disconnected from actual consequences. Soldiers who were joking in a friendly fashion with prisoners at one moment might be ordered to kill or torture them the next, without feeling any of the human warmth they had been expressing moments before. What Jünger was describing in the "second, colder consciousness" is, of course, a world of "happenings" but not of being; of families without clear affiliations; of events but not of meaning; of aggression but not of injury; a world of fictions, but not of actual social relations. Today we all live in this cold world some of the time. Some people live there permanently. Our society imitates the fiction that everything is a fiction. This can be observed at the core of personality and social relations. It shines forth throughout these pages and in many aspects of our society not examined here, such as the theories of the deconstructionists, which take any text—literary or cultural—only as a fiction to be manipulated by the critic (who sees himself as wiser); the plays of Sam Shepard, which generally allow for choice only between fictitious reality or none at all; or various novels, from those of Borges onward, which portray existence as a puzzle to be invented, and then provisionally—but no more than provisionally—solved.

The persons whom we have considered, too, seem to me to be the faces that we meet everywhere—from New York's Broadway, where Sammler saw them, to little towns in the Midwest, where Vonnegut's Harry and Helene lived. In my consulting room, at my university office, in shops, at political meetings, everywhere I am reminded of Arthur, Terry, Peter, Melissa, and the others. As for the Arthur Bremers, David Chapmans, and John Hinckleys—we read about them with all-too-distressing regularity in our newspapers.

Christopher Lasch characterized contemporary society as the "culture of narcissism." His analysis is acute and deserves widespread recognition. Narcissism—a developmental deficit resulting from inadequate early mirroring—is causally in the background of our culture, but it is a derivative and not the informing drive of the culture itself. Narcissism is merely one way of describing a personality that has become fictional to itself and seeks reflections in every glass. Perhaps Lasch did not go far enough. Our society is composed according to the belief that the self is fictive, society is theater, and events have no meaning beyond their performances. Anyone can be or become anything, because all is fraudulent and everyone is an impostor. Many people seem to want to appropriate another name—on a shirt, above the heart, or on the seat of his or her pants. We even label our psychological problems with fictions: "The Cinderella Complex," "The Peter Pan Syndrome." Indeed contemporary culture seems pervaded by fictions.

What we are seeing—what I have been describing—is the transformation of the individual and society through the fictions infused into both. Fictive personality is the psychology of our time. Fictive social relations dominate our culture.

# Epilogue:
# Understanding
# Martians

My patient Mack's treatment appeared to be going nowhere. Every time he seemed about to reveal a clue to his personality and I made a comment, he would respond flatly: "Don't you know that I am a Martian?"

I didn't have the faintest idea what being "a Martian" meant—I only knew that a wall came up when Mack said it, and his inner life was hidden. Perhaps he was saying something like, "Look, Jay, we're on different planets!" But I also felt there had to be more than this. He told me what he was, but he wouldn't tell me what this meant. In many ways he was a "perfect" psychoanalytic patient; he spoke freely, he recalled dreams, he "behaved." The only problem was that nothing happened in his analysis.

Then, one evening as I was watching television, I began

to see what he meant. As I watched a dramatization of a segment of Ray Bradbury's novel *The Martian Chronicles*, I saw what Mack felt about himself. In Bradbury's book, the crucial episode occurs in a chapter titled "September 2005: The Martian."

An old couple's son Tom has died. He is buried. The father and mother, who live in the country, are still grieving when suddenly their son Tom appears in the yard. He greets them casually and cordially. How can their dead son be alive? The old couple have to doubt their eyes, even though they could wish for nothing more than that their son be alive again. The father questions the boy, but all "Tom" can say is: "Why ask questions? Accept me!" The father, however, is unable to do so.

> "Who are you, really? You can't be Tom, but you are someone. Who?"
>
> "Don't." Startled, the boy put his hands to his face.
>
> "You can tell me," said the old man. "I'll understand. You're a Martian, aren't you? I've heard tales of the Martians: nothing definite. Stories about how rare Martians are and when they come among us they come as Earth Men. There's something about you—you're Tom and yet you're not."
>
> "Why can't you accept me and stop talking?" cried the boy. His hands completely shielded his face. "Don't doubt, please don't doubt me!"

After a while the couple takes the boy with them when they go shopping in town. He begs them not to force him to go. When they get there the boy disappears. Later, the old man hears that a lost female child has been found by another grieving couple. The old man seeks out the girl, knowing and fearing what he will find. Yes, the girl explains, she *was* Tom: now she is Lavinia. She was Tom when the old couple's desire shaped her so; now she has an identity that responds to another's desire.

Eventually, the whole town pursues the figure. Each person's desire and dream imposes a new identity on the Martian until "the swift figure . . . [means] everything to them— all identities, all persons, all names, an image reflected from ten thousand mirrors, ten thousand eyes, [a] . . . running dream."

My thoughts went to Mack. This might explain why the analysis, otherwise so "perfect," seemed to be going nowhere. Mack was playing the role of the perfect analysand, but occasionally he had told me in secret language that it *was* a role, and I was analyzing a fiction. He had read Ray Bradbury—but long before his reading he knew all too well what it was like to be a shape-shifting Martian.

Until I saw the television program based on Bradbury's novel I could only make rough attempts to interpret Mack's claim to be a Martian. I'd say: "I guess your own self seems as remote as another planet." Or, "Trying to analyze yourself must make you feel you are talking about someone else." Or, figuring that "Martian" might be a pun on my name: "You mean you just want to play the roles that I—Dr. Martin—give you, and be a perfect person, but not Mack." Sometimes I'd say simply: "I'd like to know how you became a Martian." Mack's silence then seemed to indicate that I had violated a mutual agreement that I could not understand him.

But after I understood Mack's reference to Bradbury, and told him frankly what I had learned, he started to dredge up childhood memories, old associations, fragments of wishes, dreams, daydreams, former hurts. Once I had encountered and perhaps even accepted the Martian in him, he revealed glimpses of a real self.

His case is like those of many another person treated in this book. He saved himself by learning how to play parts assigned to him. Now he is still learning how to be someone other than a Martian—ultimately to be himself.

As the author of this book, I still have much to learn

about the varieties and manifold uses of fiction. But two things I do know: It is neither possible nor desirable to dispense with fictions. But to possess *only* fictions means to be possessed by them. However many roles we play for others, we must play as few as possible for ourselves.

# Notes

## Chapter 1

## Chapter 2

*page*
51   "See that living legend": Caplan, p. 59.
51   psychiatrist William T. Carpenter: "Psychiatrist: Hinckley Mentally Ill at Time of Shooting," *Santa Ana Register*, May 15, 1982, p. A8.
53   approached him for autographs: "Hinckley Shocked by Jury Verdict," *Santa Ana Register*, June 29, 1982, p. A5.
55   Paul Zimmerman: Interview with Georgia Brown, "Screen Writing Is Like the Priesthood," *American Film*, November 1982, pp. 72–73.
55   Indeed, it was reported: Andrew Sarris, "Films in Focus: 'King of Comedy'," *Village Voice*, February 15, 1983, p. 45; see also Dale Pollock, "To Scorcese, 'Comedy' is Not Funny," *Los Angeles Times*, March 15, 1983, pp. 1, 5; Mark Jacobson, "Pictures of Marty," *Rolling Stone*, April 14, 1983, pp. 42ff; Carrie Richey, "Marty," *American Film*, November 1982, pp. 66ff; and J. Hoberman, "King of Outsiders," *Village Voice*, February 15, 1983, pp. 37ff.

## Chapter 3

57   "What a glorious opportunity": J. L. Dusseau, *"Tertium Quid*: A Third Something in a Muddled Puzzle," *Perspectives in Biology & Medicine* 25 (1982): p. 243.
57   "They can gas me": "Those Dangerous Loners," *Time*, April 13, 1981, p. 21.
58   "I am the famous Carlos": Christopher Dobson and Ronald Payne, *The Carlos Complex: A Pattern of Violence* (London: Hodder and Stoughton, 1977), p. 89.
58   Frederick J. Hacker: *Crusaders, Criminals, Crazies: Terror and Terrorism in Our Time* (New York: W. W. Norton, 1976), p. 297.
59   "Terrorism is theater": Dobson and Payne, p 15. See also Stephen Sloan, *Simulating Terrorism* (Norman, Okla.: University of Oklahoma Press, 1981).
59   One of the Arab terrorists explained: Dobson and Payne, 15–16.
60   Kreisky said nervously: Ovid Demaris, *Brothers in Blood: The International Terrorist Network* (New York: Charles Scribner's Sons, 1977), pp. 11, 13; Alex P. Schmid and Jenny de Graaf, *Violence as Communication: Insurgent Terrorism and the Western News Media* (London and Beverly Hills: Sage Publications, 1982), p. 33; Christopher Dobson and Ronald Payne, *The Terrorists: Their Weapons, Leaders, and Tactics*, rev. ed. (New York: Facts on File, 1982); Walter Laqueur, ed., *The Terrorism Reader* (New York: New American Library, 1978).
62   "Stockholm Syndrome": "What is happening to the Hostages in Teheran?" *Psychiatric Annals* 10 (May 1980): pp. 186–189. See also Perry Ottenberg, "Terrorism: 'No Hostages are Innocent'," *Psychiatric Annals* 10 (May 1980): pp. 179–85.
63   "The media princess": Hacker, pp. 143–144.
64   "I did not have the slightest idea": Patricia Campbell Hearst, with Alvin Moscow, *Every Secret Thing* (Garden City, N.Y.: Doubleday & Co., 1982), pp. 11–12.
64   "As the flashbulbs": Hearst and Moscow, p. 379.
66   In 1983, FBI Director: Anthony DeStefano, "Perilous Work," *Wall Street Journal*, November 4, 1985, pp. 1, 14.

page

68  Robert C. Tucker: *Stalin as Revolutionary* (New York: W. W. Norton, 1973); "A Stalin Biographer's Memoir," *Introspection in Biography*, eds. Samuel H. Baron and Carl Pletsch (Hillsdale, N.J. and London: The Analytic Press, 1985), pp. 249–72.

68  *Neurosis and Human Growth* (New York: W. W. Norton, 1950).

71  "a militant pacifist": John le Carré, *The Little Drummer Girl* (New York: Alfred A. Knopf, 1983), pp. 79; also quoted: pp. 39ff. 398, 415.

## Chapter 4

76  Henry Adams: "Buddha and Brahma," *Yale Review* 5 (1915): p. 88.

77  a still photograph from *The Wizard of Oz:* James R. Gaines, "The Man Who Shot Lennon," *People*, February 23, 1987, p. 65.

77  Nancy C. A. Roeske: *American Journal of Psychiatry* 138 (January 1981): p. 139.

78  Canto V of the *Inferno: The Divine Comedy of Dante Alighieri*, trans. Melville Best Anderson (New York: The Heritage Press, 1944), pp. 22–23.

79  Waldo Frank expresses it well: Preface to Miguel Cervantes, *Don Quixote de la Mancha*, trans. Samuel Putnam (New York: Viking, 1949), p. vi; also quoted: pp. 16, 27, 29, 17.

81  In 1937 Helene Deutsch: *Neuroses and Character Types* (New York: International Universities Press, 1965), pp. 218–19, 221.

82  Freud wrote in 1905: *Jokes and Their Relation to the Unconscious*, Standard Edition of the Complete Psychological Works of Sigmund Freud, trans. James Strachey, vol. 8 (New York: W. W. Norton, 1st ed. 1966; reprint 1981), p. 232n.

83  "I enjoy no single": Johann Wolfgang von Goethe, *The Sorrows of Young Werther* (1774), in *Great German Short Novels and Stories* (New York: Random House, 1952), p. 60; also quoted: pp. 96, 99, 134.

83  "I had not yet found a friend": Jean-Jacques Rousseau, *The New Heloise*, in *The Indispensable Rousseau*, ed. J. H. Mason (London: Quartet Books, 1979).

84  George Brandes: *Goethe*, trans. Andrew W. Porterfield (New York: Crown, 1936), pp. 214–15.

85  Graham Greene, in *Monsignor Quixote:* (New York: Washington Square Press, 1983; [1st ed., Simon & Schuster, 1982]), pp. 14–15.

86  "We must take into account": Luigi Pirandello, *Henry IV*, in *Naked Masks: Five Plays*, ed. Eric Bentley (New York: E. P. Dutton, 1958), pp. 174, 189, 191, 204–205.

87  "The Kugelmass Episode": Woody Allen, in *The New Yorker*, May 2, 1977, pp. 34–39.

## Chapter 5

92  "Miss Q": Nagera, *Female Sexuality and the Oedipus Complex* (New York: Aronson, 1975), pp. 91–92.

102  "Creative Writers and Day-Dreaming": Sigmund Freud, Standard Edition, vol. 9, pp. 149–50.

104  Dr. Raymond D. Fowler: "The Case of the Multicolored Personality," *Psychology Today* 20 (November 1986): pp. 38–49.

*page*
106        William Butler Yeats: Richard Ellmann, *Yeats, The Man and the Masks* (New York: W. W. Norton, 1979, 1978; New York: E. P. Dutton, 1948) pp. 171–76.

## Chapter 6

107        "The thing I resent": Maureen Dowd, "Testing Himself," *New York Times Magazine*, September 28, 1986.
108        Again and again in his book: Constantin Stanislavski, *An Actor's Handbook*, ed. and trans. Elizabeth Reynolds Hapgood (New York: Theatre Arts Books, 1903), pp. 56, 73, 121–222, 159.
109        method acting being challenged: Mimi Kramer, "Beyond Method Acting," *The New Criterion* 5 (September 1986): pp. 67–78.
110        "She would get some music": West, *The Day of the Locust* (New York: New Directions, 1950 [1st ed., 1940]), p. 60.
110        "I'm Rita Hayworth": R. D. Laing, *The Divided Self* (Harmondsworth, U.K.: Penquin, 1965 [1st ed., 1959]), p. 203.
110        "to play the part of Buffalo Bill": W. F. Cody, *The Life and Adventures of "Buffalo Bill"* (New York: John Wiley & Sons, 1927), pp. 248, 258.
111        In 1979, an updated version: S. Marowitz, "Myth and Realism in Recent Criticism of the American Literary West," *Journal of American Studies* 15 (1981): pp. 95–114.
112        Sally Field, in an interview: Elizabeth Darcy, "I've Stopped Pretending to be a Good Girl," *McCall's*, October 1984, pp. 14, 22.
115        "I can be as demanding": David Rosenthal, "Meryl Streep: Stepping In and Out of Roles," *Rolling Stone*, October 15, 1981, p. 17.
115        "Call me in six years:" Charles Champlain, " 'Sophie's' on Location in Flatbush," *Los Angeles Times Calendar*, May 16, 1982, p. 28; see also Steven X. Rea, "Meryl Streep Talks About 'Sophie's Choice,' " *The Movie Magazine*, 1982, pp. 4ff.
116        Peter Sellers was the son: Alexander Walker, *Peter Sellers: The Authorized Biography*, Preface by Lynne Frederick Sellers (New York: Macmillan, 1984), pp. xiv–xv, 17–18, 32, 35–36, 58, 82–83, 96–198, 102–105, 112–114, 121–122, 131, 139.
119        In the fall of 1980: Eleanor Antin, *Being Antinova* (Los Angeles: Astro Artz, 1983), pp. 6, 11, 20–21, 80.
122        "Did Chouang dream": Conrad Aiken, "A Letter from Li Po," *Collected Poems 1916–1970*, Second edition (New York: Oxford University Press, 1970), p. 907.

## Chapter 7

127        Recently, Joyce McDougall: *Theaters of the Mind: Illusion and Truth on the Psychoanalytic Stage* (New York: Basic Books, 1985), pp. 3–4.
129        "Fictions," as he uses the term: Hans Vaihinger, *The Philosophy of "As If"*, trans. C. K. Ogden (New York: Harcourt, Brace, 1911), pp. 84, 215, 354–55.
130        Donald Spence: *Narrative Truth and Historical Truth* (New York: W. W. Norton, 1982), p. 137.

*page*

130 Alfred Adler acknowledged: *The Individual Psychology of Alfred Adler: A Systematic Presentation*, ed. Heinz L. Ansbacher and Rowena R. Ansbacher (New York: Basic Books, 1956), pp. 76, 93.

131 In 1942 Helene Deutsch: *Neuroses and Character Types*, pp. 262–66.

132 The clearest work on schizoid: Harry Guntrip, *Schizoid Phenomena, Object Relations and the Self* (New York: International Universities Press, 1968), pp. 18, 59.

134 R. D. Laing: pp. 95, 70–71.

134 Freud had said in 1911: "Psycho-Analytic Notes on an Autobiographical Account of a Case of Paranoia," Standard Edition, vol. 12, pp. 70, 77.

135 After Bruno Kreisky: Demaris, *Brothers in Blood*, p. 11.

136 Anna Freud as "altruistic surrender": *The Ego and the Mechanisms of Defense* (New York: International Universities Press, 1966), p. 125.

137 Kris in 1956: "The Personal Myth," pp. 272, 284–85.

137 Kohut argues: *The Restoration of the Self* (New York, International Universities Press, 1977). See also: *The Analysis of the Self* (New York: International Universities Press, 1971), and Kohut and Ernest Wolf, "The Disorders of the Self and Their Treatment: An Outline," *International Journal of Psycho-Analysis* 59 (1978): pp. 413–26.

139 Long before Kohut, Freud: "Fetishism," Standard Edition, vol. 21, pp. 152–58.

140 Michael Franz Basch: "The Perception of Reality and the Disavowal of Meaning," *The Annual of Psychoanalysis* 11 (1983): p. 135.

140 Erik Erikson wrote: Erikson, *Identity and the Life Cycle* (New York: W. W. Norton, 1980; New York: International Universities Press, 1959), p. 22.

141 The French psychoanalyst André Green: *Narcissisme de vie. Narcissisme de mort* (Paris: Minuit, 1983). See also Green, *The Tragic Effect*, trans. Alan Sheridan (Cambridge: Cambridge University Press, 1979), p. 179.

143 Harris, Hearst writes: Hearst and Moscow, pp. 268–69.

144 Janine Chasseguet-Smirgel's book *Creativity and Perversion* (New York and London: W. W. Norton, 1984).

145 Laing's case of David: *Divided Self*, pp. 72–73.

147 her 1956 essay on the imposter: Deutsch, "The Imposter: Contributions to Ego Psychology of a Psychopath," *Neuroses and Character Types*, pp. 319–38.

148 Anna Freud, too: *Ego and the Mechanisms of Defense*, p. 132.

148 Kohut's first psychoanalytic paper: "*Death in Venice* by Thomas Mann: A Story About the Disintegration of Artistic Sublimation" (1957) in *Search for the Self*, vol. 1, ed. Paul Ornstein (New York: International Universities Press, 1975), pp. 107–30.

## Chapter 8

154 Stern cites a clinical instance: Daniel N. Stern, *The Interpersonal World of the Infant: A View from Psychoanalysis and Developmental Biology* (New York: Basic Books, 1985), pp. 211–13.

*page*
156     These occur at two months: Robert N. Emde and James F. Sorce, "The Rewards of Infancy: Emotional Availability and Maternal Referencing," *Frontiers of Infant Psychiatry*, eds. Justin D. Call, Eleanor Galenson, & Robert L. Tyson (New York: Basic Books, 1983), pp. 17–30.

156     "transitional phenomena": D. W. Winnicott, "Transitional Objects and Transitional Phenomena" in *Collected Papers* (New York: Basic Books, 1953).

157     "The reading of storybooks": Margaret Mahler, F. Pine, and A. Bergman, *The Psychological Birth of the Human Infant* (New York: Basic Books, 1975), p. 100.

157     "his mother would not come": Anna Freud and D. Burlingham, *Infants Without Families* (New York: International Universities Press, 1973 [1st ed., 1944]), p. 441.

158     Esther Bick: "The Experience of the Skin in Early Object Relations," *International Journal of Psycho-Analysis* 49 (1968): pp. 484–86.

161     "Munchausen's Syndrome": R. Asher, "Munchausen Syndrome," *Lancet* 1 (1951): pp. 339–41; J. C. Baker, "Hospital and Operation Addiction," *British Journal of Clinical Practice* 20 (1966): p. 63; P. Justus *et al.*, "Probing the Dynamics of Munchausen's Syndrome," *Annals of International Medicine* 73 (1980): pp. 120–27; Karl Menninger, "Polysurgery and Polysurgery Addiction," *Psychoanalytic Quarterly* 3 (1934): p. 173; H. R. Spiro, "Chronic Facticious Illness," *Archives of General Psychiatry* 18 (1968): pp. 569–79; D. A. Swanson, "The Munchausen Syndrome," *American Journal of Psychotherapy* 35 (1981): pp. 436–43.

166     Peter, a young patient: Justin D. Call, "Hallucinosis and *The Wizard of Oz:* Psychosis in Childhood," copyright 1975 by Justin D. Call, M.D.

## Chapter 9

175     Sartre's autobiography *The Words:* Jean-Paul Sartre (New York: Braziller, 1964), 15–60, 69–75.

176     "The only thing I can say": Jean-Paul Sartre, *Nausea*, trans. Lloyd Alexander (New York: New Directions, 1964 [1st ed., 1938]), p. 2.

177     Sartre went far beyond: See Philip Thody, *Sartre: A Biographical Introduction* (New York: Charles Scribner's Sons, 1971), p. 76; *Action*, December 19, 1944; Joseph Halpern, *Critical Fictions: The Literary Criticism of Jean-Paul Sartre* (New Haven & London: Yale University Press, 1976), and Douglas Collins, *Sartre as Biographer* (Cambridge, Mass.: Harvard University Press, 1980).

177     Bela Grunberger: *Le Narcissisme* (Paris: Payot, 1971).

177     "Before I sat down to write *Taxi Driver:* Richard Thompson, "Writer Paul Schrader," *Film Comment*, March–April 1976, p. 11.

178     As a general, George S. Patton: Martin Blumenson, *Patton: The Man Behind the Legend, 1885–1945* (New York: William Morrow, 1985), *passim*.

181     a remarkable dream: *The Wolf-Man by the Wolf-Man*, ed. Muriel Gardiner (New York: Basic Books, 1971), p. 173; Freud, Standard Edition, vol. 17, p. 29.

*page*
182   what Roy Schafer says: *Language and Insight* (New Haven: Yale University Press, 1978).
182   Otto Rank wrote: William Offenkrantz and Arnold Tobin, "Problems of the Therapeutic Alliance: Freud and the Wolf Man," *International Journal of Psycho-Analysis* 54 (1973): pp. 75–78.
182   Freud wrote to his patient: "Letters Pertaining to Freud's 'History of an Infantile Neurosis'," *Psychoanalytic Quarterly* 26 (1957): pp. 449–60.
182   The Wolf Man wrote back in haste: Wolfman's letter of June 6, 1926, quoted in *Psychoanalytic Quarterly*, pp. 458–59.
183   "So long as he": Ruth Mack Brunswick, "A Supplement to Freud's 'History of an Infantile Neurosis' " (1928), in *The Wolf-Man by the Wolf-Man*, pp. 263–307; quoted: pp. 284–85, 264–65, 269, 271, 274, 278.
185   Gogol's description: "The Nose," *The Diary of a Madman and Other Stories*, trans. Andrew R. MacAndrew (New York: New American Library, 1960), pp. 33, 34; and *passim*. See also Mark Kanzer, "Gogol—A Study on Wit and Paranoia," *Journal of the American Psychoanalytic Association* 3 (1955): pp. 110–25.

## Chapter 10

188   "a simple skeleton": Malcolm Cowley, *The Faulkner-Cowley File: Letters and Memories, 1944–1962* (New York: Viking, 1966), p. 114.
188   born of a Negro and an alligator: John Faulkner, *My Brother Bill: An Affectionate Reminiscence* (New York: Trident, 1963), pp. 172–73.
188   John Faulkner writes: *My Brother Bill*, pp. 10–11.
189   "I was suddenly taken": Joseph Blotner, *Faulkner: A Biography* (New York: Random House, 1974), vol. 1, pp. 65–66. Blotner's two-volume biography is the source of most biographical details in the following account, along with books by Cowley, John Faulkner, and Murry C. Falkner. See also Michael Grimwood, *Heart in Conflict: Faulkner's Struggles with Vocation* (Athens, Georgia and London: University of Georgia Press, 1987).
191   his brother Murry recalled: Murry C. Falkner, *The Falkners of Mississippi* (Baton Rouge: Louisiana State University Press, 1967), pp. 26–27.
192   "I want to be a writer," Murry Falkner, p. 6.
192   "I more or less grew up": Cowley, p. 67.
192   "We lived under": John Faulkner, pp. 81–82.
192   "Don't Complain": Blotner, vol. 1, p. 79.
193   "Like a corset": John Faulkner, pp. 81–82.
194   "on the humiliating grounds": Pamela R. Broughton, "Faulkner's Cubist Novels," in *A Cosmos of My Own: Faulkner and Yoknapatawpha*, eds. D. Fowler and A. J. Abadie (Jackson: University Press of Mississippi, 1981), p. 68.
196   The psychoanalyst Harvey Strauss: personal communication.
197   This is, as Faulkner's authorized: vol. 1, p. 541.
197   He wrote, he said: Carvel Collins, ed., *William Faulkner: Early Prose and Poetry* (Boston: Little, Brown, 1962), p. 115.
198   a "touchstone": Blotner, vol. 1, pp. 531–32.

## Chapter 11

page
200    "Here's a surprise": Ernest Jones, *The Life and Work of Sigmund Freud*, vol. 3: *The Last Phase, 1919–1939* (New York: Basic Books, 1957), p. 418.
201    "I was trained": Jones, vol. 3, p. 418.
201    As recently as 1985: Harry Trosman, *Freud and the Imaginative World* (Hillsdale, N.J. and London: The Analytic Press, 1985), p. xi.
202    "torn [him] up by the roots": Sigmund Freud, *The Origins of Psycho-Analysis. Letters to Wilhelm Fliess, Drafts and Notes: 1887–1902* (New York: Basic Books, 1954), pp. 210–11.
204    Joyce McDougall: pp. 185–86.
204    The French psychoanalyst J. L. Pontalis: "Between the Dream as Object and the Dream-Text," *Frontiers in Psychoanalysis* (New York: International Universities Press), p. 33.
204    "I shall proceed": *The Interpretation of Dreams* (1900), Standard Edition, vol. 4, p. 105.
205    The dream of Irma's injection begins: the dream is analyzed by Freud in *The Interpretation of Dreams*, Standard Edition, vol. 4, pp. 106–21.
205    Max Schur: "Some Additional 'Day Residues' of the 'Specimen Dream of Psychoanalysis'," *Psychoanalysis—A General Psychology*, eds. Rudolf Loewenstein, *et al* (New York: International Universities Press, 1966), pp. 45–85; quoted concerning Freud and Fleiss, p. 58.
209    a novel by Fritz Reuter: Alexander Grinstein, *Sigmund Freud's Dreams* (New York International Universities Press, 1980). Grinstein's book on Freud's use of fictions in dreams and dream-associations is a very important study and has significantly influenced my investigation of Freud's fictive processes throughout this chapter.
212    In 1934: Giovanni Papini, "A Visit to Freud," *Freud as We Knew Him*, ed. Hendrik Ruitenbeck (Detroit: Wayne State University Press, 1973), pp. 98–102; pp. 99–101 quoted.

## Chapter 12

214    Dorothy Lee, an anthropologist: Dorothy Lee, "The Conception of the Self Among the Wintu Indians," *Freedom and Culture* (Englewood Cliffs, N.J.: Prentice-Hall, 1959; 1st ed., 1950), pp. 134, 140.
216    A young woman told one investigator: John L. Caughey, "Artificial Social Relations in Modern America," *American Quarterly* 30 (1978): p. 72. The entire essay (pp. 70–89) is provocative, and I have drawn freely upon it in my analysis.
217    A first novel published in 1982: Meg Wolitzer, *Sleepwalking* (New York: Random House, 1982).
218    In *The Modern Temper*, Joseph Wood Krutch (New York: Harcourt, Brace, 1929), p. 176.
220    The cultural anthropologist John L. Caughey has cited: "Artificial Social Relations in Modern America," pp. 87–88; quotation from p. 87.
221    the average american child": quoted in Melvin DeFleur, *Theories of Communication* (New York: McKay, 1970), p. 136.

page
222 By age eighteen: Pamela Cantor, "Anger May Be a Signal of Too Much TV," *Los Angeles Times*, Aug. 23, 1986.

222 An average of five acts of violence: David Pearl, *et al.*, eds., *Television and Behavior: Ten Years of Scientific Progress and Implications for the Eighties*, vol. 2 (Rockville, Maryland: National Institute of Mental Health, 1982), p. 169.

223 We hear that five Croatian men: Schmid and de Graaf, *Violence as Communication*, pp. 34–35, 36.

223 A copycat skyjacker: Hacker, *Crusaders, Criminals, Crazies*, pp. 28–29.

223 Since the publication in 1972: David Pearl, *Television and Behavior*, vol. 1, p. 111.

224 In a five-year study: E. D. McCarthy, *et al.*, "Violence and Behavior Disorders," *Journal of Communication* 25 (1975): pp 71–85.

224 Two other studies: T. M. Williams, "Differential Impact of TV on Children: A Natural Experiment in Communities With and Without TV," Paper presented at the International Society for Research on Aggression, Washington, D.C., 1978; G. Granszberg and J. Steinberg, "Television and the Canadian Indian," Technical Report, Department of Anthropology, University of Winnipeg, 1980.

224 The surprising result of these studies: David Pearl, *Television and Behavior*, vol. 1, p. 37.

225 "Events became socially effective": Hacker, *Crusaders, Criminals, Crazies*, p. 161.

226 "Watching too much television": "Answers from John Hinckley," *Newsweek*, Oct. 12, 1981, p. 50.

226 Crime and detective stories: R. Garry, "Television's Impact on the Child," *Children on TV: Television's Impact on the Child* (Washington, D.C.: Association for Childhood International, 1967).

226 Other researchers asked: J. M. Quarforth, "Children's Understanding of the Nature of Television Characters," *Journal of Communication* 29 (1979): pp. 210–18.

226 "they're lowered down on a rope": B. S. Greenberg and B. Reeves, "Children and the Perceived Reality of Television," *Journal of Social Issues* 32 (1976): pp. 86–97; "Children's Perception of Television Characters," *Human Communication Research* 3 (1977): pp. 113–27.

226 Especially under conditions: G. Noble, *Children in Front of the Small Screen* (London: Constable, 1975).

227 The great German writer: Ernst Jünger, "Uber den Schmerz," *Blätter und Sterne* (Hamburg: Hanseatische Verlagsanstalt, 1942); translation quoted from Erich Kahler, *The Tower and the Abyss* (New York: Viking, 1967 [1st ed., 1957]), pp. 89–97.

228 Christopher Lasch characterized: *The Culture of Narcissism* (New York: W. W. Norton, 1978).

## Epilogue

231 In Bradbury's book: Ray Bradbury, *The Martian Chronicles* (New York: Bantam Books, 1979, [1st ed., 1950]), pp. 119–31.

# Index

Boldface headings indicate fictional characters.

# Index

255

may form an "idealized image" of himself or herself—that is to say, the child creates a fiction, a superman image, of his perfection. If the inner pressure of anxiety continues over a long duration, this self-idealizing defense will gradually evolve into an "idealized self," an image and imaginary or fictive identity—*not* the real identity, but a fiction of one. What Horney calls the "search for glory" consists of the attempt to force the world to acknowledge the "idealized self" as the real self.

Horney, then, is describing the creation of a rigid self as a protection against basic fear. Such a self, if it is to be truly protective, can have no flaws, no human limitations. The shield must be invulnerable. Others must also accept and adore the "idealized self," or the protection is threatened. But others, whose adulation is so desperately needed, must also be scorned. *They* are fallible, merely human, potential adulators, but otherwise insignificant. The "idealized self" is a grandiose conception. The "idealized self" is right; all others are wrong—and their errors are threatening to the perfect world that could be created should the idealized self attain the power to suppress others and have its own way. The self-hatred and fears that are repressed and disavowed by self-idealization inevitably are projected onto others— they, in their humanness, are to be hated; they are to be feared. To protect itself fully, Horney writes, the idealized self must achieve a "vindictive triumph" over any persons who might in some way question the supremacy of the idealized self and its values.

Tucker applied this thesis to the cult of personality that formed around Stalin. "What if," he asked himself, "the idealized image of Stalin, appearing day after day in the party-controlled, party-supervised press, were *an idealized self in Horney's sense?*" Stalin would then be like many other neurotics, except that he possessed political power unprecedented in history. "In that case, the Stalin cult must reflect

Stalin's own monstrously inflated vision of himself as the greatest genius of Russian and world history. The cult must be an institutionalization of his neurotic character structure." Things fell into place. Stalin's ruthless suppression of colleagues, his infusion of himself into all institutions of Soviet society, his inability to tolerate dissent, all pointed to a drive toward mastery through the elimination of all values but his own. He had, Tucker concluded, used his enormous power to gain almost total control, mobilizing the resources of a totalitarian state to repress his "enemies," to scorn mere human claims, and to install himself as the central ideal and all-wise hero of an entire society.

To defend against a basic dread, young Stalin learned to make a fiction about himself. Then, during the revolution, he found a body of materials by which he could shape himself: the writings of Marx, Lenin, and others, along with the romance of the revolution, all gave him purpose and an image of himself as powerful, so special a person that he could help to overthrow a czar and then replace Lenin, the father of the revolution. Thus the boy Josif Dzhugashvili, subjected to a dismal early life and repeatedly beaten by his drunken father, found a new family in communism and a new family name, "Stalin," man of steel. He would rescue Russia from victimization by the czar, as if the czar were a bad drunken father who beat his children. But beneath the defenses provided by the fictions of "The Revolutionary" still festered the old anxiety, self-doubts, anger at authority, and hatred of rivals that led to the young Stalin's anger in the first place.

This, indeed, was Nikita Khrushchev's view as expressed in his secret report to the Twentieth Party Congress, printed in *The New York Times* as "On the Cult of Personality and its Consequences." In this document Khrushchev depicted Stalin as grandiose, insecure, subject to rages, requiring continuous reassurance, arrogant but uncertain, insatiably hun-

was right that his success and the more permissive environment of the university had encouraged him to make the
attempt at being whole. But his mother's letter had shattered
that, reasserting forcefully what he had been taught as a
child: that bad thoughts led to bad actions. Her letter said,
in essence, that his hidden self was a crazy, sinful being
that should be rooted out.

Analysis helped to provide a new forum by which Thomas
could again make the attempt at self-integration. Encouraged
to relax, Thomas at first refused to lie down; but he did
begin to associate freely and to say whatever came into his
mind. The battle between his associations and his superego
prohibitions and inhibitions soon followed: he should not
be thinking such and such a thought, the analyst would
punish him, throw him out of treatment, think ill of him,
and so on. But then, he might add defensively, his thoughts
were not really his—he was a good person, his thoughts
came from his double or a little voice inside him, and so
on. The goal of treatment, he argued, should be to get these
bad thoughts out; that goal actually helped him to associate
freely, as if the bad selves inside him could be emptied
like water from a bucket. Over and over he had to be told
that his fantasies were normal and acceptable to the analyst;
and that, moreover, he would not be obliged to act upon
them. This made him believe that the analyst was deceiving
him, tempting him, and encouraging him to regard his hidden
self as all right, but would then attack him after he had
wholly revealed himself. When the anticipated attack didn't
occur, Thomas made tentative efforts to bring out more and
more of his guilty secrets. Eventually, he began to feel like
a "real" person.

The only problem was that his writing, of all kinds, had
come to a halt. His writings on literary theory and experimen-
tal poetry and fiction had come from his imitation of his
father; his popular fiction had come from his split-off self.

When these two selves were linked, he seemed to lose the drives that had produced his writing—a kind of secular preaching, or anti-preaching—and he was now generally content with his life and family except for the fact that he was no longer writing. This left him depressed, since authorship, at the level of the ego, had become a part of his self-esteem. After a "dry" period, he began writing again—but not nearly so compulsively—in an interdisciplinary field that incorporated and fused together most of the elements of his previously divided interests.

In what way do authors identify with the characters they create? Or, to put it another way, how do characters reflect the author? Freud took up these questions in his best-known essay on literary productions, "Creative Writers and Day-Dreaming," of 1908. At the end of his essay he comments on the egocentric aspect of literary creation. "One feature above all cannot fail to strike us about the creations of these story writers," he remarks. "Each of them has a hero who is the centre of interest, for whom the writer tries to win our sympathy by every possible means and whom he seems to place under the protection of a special Providence." This, Freud indicates, is not merely literary convention: rather, the very idea of the central hero originally arises from the importance of preserving the ego. "Through the revealing characteristic of invulnerability," Freud writes, "we can immediately recognize His Majesty the Ego, the hero alike of every day-dream and every story." Freud makes the basic distinction between the active aspect of the ego, represented in the dynamic hero, and the passive components of the ego, often appearing as the hero who is a spectator to the events of the story. Further splitting may occur, he also suggests, in assigning different parts of the ego—and superego—to various characters, then watching them work out externally the same drama that is always occurring inside.